100 IDEAS
FOR TEACHING LITERACY

CONTINUUM ONE HUNDREDS

Also Available from Continuum

100+ Ideas for Teaching English – Angella Cooze

100 Ideas for Assemblies: Primary School Edition – Fred Sedgwick

100 Ideas for Developing Thinking in the Primary School – Fred Sedgwick

101 Essential Lists for Primary Teachers – Fred Sedgwick

Foundations of Literacy – Sue Palmer and Ros Bayley

Teaching Poetry – Fred Sedgwick

100 IDEAS
FOR TEACHING
LITERACY

Fred Sedgwick

continuum

Continuum International Publishing Group

The Tower Building   80 Maiden Lane
11 York Road   Suite 704, New York
London, SE1 7NX   NY 10038

www.continuumbooks.com

British Library Cataloguing-in-Publication Data
A catalogue record for this book is available from the British
Library.

ISBN: 9781847063571 (paperback)

Library of Congress Cataloging-in-Publication Data
A catalog record is available from the Library of Congress

Typeset by Newgen Imaging Systems Pvt Ltd, Chennai, India
Printed and bound in Great Britain by Ashford Colour
Press Ltd

For Daniel

By learning you will teach; by teaching you will learn
Latin proverb

CONTENTS

SECTION II   **Key Stage 1**

SECTION III   **Key Stage 2**

ACKNOWLEDGEMENTS

I am grateful to Peggy Cotton for permission to print
four lines from John Cotton's poem 'Kilroy was Here'
from the book of that name (Chatto and Windus 1975).
I am also grateful to Terri and Georgia Morgan for their
contributions, and to Daniel Sedgwick, both the child he
was and the man he is now, for his help, and for
permission to use his poem 'Dad'; and to Marga
Gibbs-van Dijk for her help with the Dutch in Idea 95,
and to Jessica Gibbs for her help with the German.

> *A perfect gentleman then neared;*
> *The wagtail, in a winking,*
> *With terror rose and disappeared;*
> *The baby fell a-thinking.*
>   Thomas Hardy 'Wagtail and Baby'

If we want to think about literacy, we had better start by thinking about thinking: our own and the children's. Hardy's baby was thinking.

I don't know of any government documents that have put thinking (or speaking or listening, either, for that matter) at the centre of the literacy, and I know why (see Reading, p. xvi below). But we, as teachers, Learning Support Assistants (LSAs) and probably parents, are better at understanding children than secretaries of state for education.

We are closer to children. We often reflect on their thinking. If we think of the children we are associated with, we remember them in their cots as they look and wonder and as they think. They think as they play with the wrapping paper round their presents at first, and then as they play with the presents; they think as they watch branches wave, and later as they watch the waves burst into life and then die on the sand; they think as they see their parents hug and kiss and talk and argue and (sometimes) split up; they think as they visit zoos, and as they listen to new sounds; they think as they watch a wagtail flying in fear from a human being; they think as they hear the news of the deaths of grandparents or great-grandparents.

So by the time the children meet us, their teachers and their LSAs (parents have already done so much) they are already thinkers. The question is: do their opportunities for thinking, and with them their opportunities for becoming more literate, improve when they go school? Do they even have chances, as the saying goes, to hear themselves think? Thinking is a central plank in our teaching of literacy. So it is central to every single part of this book.

TALKING

> *'The time has come', the Walrus said,*
> *'To talk of many things . . .'*
>> Lewis Carroll *Through the Looking-Glass*

Later, it is through talking that children's thinking takes a less provisional shape. Children can talk. Well, we know that, of course. If we are parents, we have celebrated that first 'Mum', that first 'Dad'. We have, indeed, lodged those words in our hearts. We have watched their talk develop as they play, as they visit places, as they greet their grandparents each time in more sophisticated ways. We often tell people about things 'that Daniel [or Georgia or David or Llewellyn] has just said . . .'

But here is a contradiction. In the classroom, we constantly *complain* about their talk. The most common use of the word in school, probably, is in the sentence: 'Is someone talking?' We ask it, mock-suspiciously, looking around the room with injured dignity as we look up from some vital task, calling the register, for example, or totting up 'hot dinners' against 'packed lunches'. 'I thought (!) I asked for silence'.

Sometimes, though, in our classrooms, we *want* them to talk. And they are silent. We might reflect on why this is. It may, possibly, be because they have not had chances to talk at home: that their homes are silent. Or that their homes are so noisy that they can't get a word in edgeways. That the telly is always 'blaring', and that everyone sits slumped, couch-spuddy, like the Royle family.

I don't believe either of these. These reasons are not, after all, consistent (are the children's homes silent, or are they noisy?). See Gordon Wells' book *The Meaning Makers* for a brilliant refutation of this fallacy, especially 'Rosie: A Learning-Disabled Child', pp. 94–101.

Is it (and this is far more likely) that our demands for silence in school constitute a kind of brain-washing? That 'talk' almost always conjures up 'naughtiness' in their minds? Do we give them sufficient time to talk? Or do we actually discourage it?

Is it because we don't use the same kind of language that children are accustomed to at home (and in which they are almost certainly fluent)? The nastiest example of this is the child who has been labelled very early in his school career as lacking in language: he is then faced with a test. Often this takes place in a little, featureless room, or, worse, a corridor. Either way, opposite him sits a stranger who asks him questions he has never heard before. She points to a series of pictures, the like of which he has never seen before. When he answers (if he does) she replies, at best, 'Well done David'; or perhaps she doesn't answer at all, but silently ticks a box. Whatever she does, this is a kind of interaction that is new to him. What is going on here? He must wonder.

If we do use the kind of language that the child uses at home, does that language mean the same in school as it does in the home? For example, 'Would you like some more potatoes?' is certainly a question. But is 'Would you come and sit on the carpet, please?'? They sound much the same to the child – they both begin with 'Would you . . .' and end, audibly, with a question mark. The latter is, however gently spoken, however politely expressed, not a question at all, but an order.

Children who are fluent speakers at home are often bemused (and even distressed) by school language, which is both *like* home language, and subtly *un*like it; and for that reason, among others, they become reluctant speakers; unless, of course, the school appreciates the problem and takes steps to alleviate it. I suggest ways of helping children to talk of anything, including in Foundation Stage below. There is no reason why most children should not be able

To talk of many things:
Of shoes – and ships – and sealing-wax –
Of cabbages – and kings –
And why the sea is boiling hot –
And whether pigs have wings.

LISTENING

I have seen
A curious child . . .
. . . his very soul
Listened intensely. . .

> *William Wordsworth 'The Excursion'*

Common sense, which is, as so often, wrong, suggests
that listening is merely a question of being still and silent
while someone else does something. But there are two
ways of listening: passively, making no response to what
you hear; and actively, making connections between what
you are hearing now and what you've heard before.
Wordsworth's child was doing the latter: connecting
shell-noise with the experiences he had had before. When
adults listen to a radio talk, they sometimes feel a need to
stop the talk, and listen again, and think. With children
listening to books we should be continually stopping for
thinking, re-reading, (and talking) time.

The thinking is more difficult, because it requires
periods of silence that may feel awkward. But these
intervals should be seen as opportunities for
reflection, for working out, for *thinking*, for talking.
Note that talking comes second there, after thinking.
No hands up . . . or not yet! Think!

READING

Reading maketh a full man . . .

> *Francis Bacon* Of Studies

Neither thinking nor talking can be measured; neither
can listening. That's why politicians and inspectors
(parroting government edicts) focus on reading, which,

in their scheme of things, can. They delight in placing schools in league tables in terms of reading scores (among other measurements). This necessarily entails focusing on something that we, as adults, ignore almost all the time: the mechanics of reading, phonics; or fonix, as it is phonetically. We don't, or rarely, use phonics as we read the paper, or a novel, or look at the headlines and captions on a television screen.

And this emphasis on measurement disguises a little appreciated fact: *Most children can read before they come to school.* Does this sentence feel wrong? If it does, there are two reasons for this.

We see children as helpless. They are, of course. When they are babies they can't feed themselves unaided. They can't hold up their lolling heads. We have to be in the same room with them all the time, except when they're asleep, and even then we check they're OK every so often (for the first child, anyway). Even when they begin to toddle, we have to watch them constantly in case they wander into a road, get too close to a dog, or eat something unsuitable.

But even in their cots, when they wake in the morning, they are active learners. We only have to watch his eyes as he looks around his room, or her hands and her toothless gums as she feels and tastes for new sensations; as he looks to you to renew the overpowering love he felt when he saw you last. They are thinking about what they can see and touch and taste; they are thinking about you.

And once they are getting about on their feet, both their thirst for knowledge, and for understanding of that knowledge are unquenchable. We as adults can only sorrowfully admit that thirst isn't ours any more. In *Great Expectations* by Charles Dickens, Mrs Gargery constantly complains that the young Pip is full of 'questions'. She, of course, is beyond asking questions; under the pressures of her own life (and her furious temper, of course, and her own secret) she has only time and energy to survive. Pip is still a learner; but he can read what

matters: the inscriptions on his parents' gravestones.
So he is full of questions.

The second reason why that sentence ('Most children can read before they come to school') feels wrong is the responsibility of the media and the politicians. Newspaper readers, for example, would never know about children's learning from the way columnists write about schools. For them, a large minority of children *leave*, let alone *come to* school, without being able to read. It must be true: otherwise, it isn't news. These commentators see reading as recognizing the sounds letters 'make'.

But reading is much more than that. It is an emotional and intellectual matter. I have just read a news story about the murder of a baby; another about the election of a new president of the United States; another about my team winning 1-0 away from home, and not for a second did I detach my emotional being, nor my intellectual one, from what I was reading. Not once did I use phonics: one of the football players is called Shumulikovski: I simply reduced his name, temporarily, to 'Shumu'.

Children do the same. They have their strategies for understanding words. They recognize whole words; they look at context.

'Children can': that sentence, or other sentences expressing the same thought, will come up many times in this book. Within certain constraints – not many of them – children will learn better the more we *expect* them to.

WRITING

> . . . *Writing an exact man.*
>
> *Francis Bacon, again*

I teach writing all over the country. Sometimes the teacher tells me: 'Our reading scores are good, but our writing is a problem'.

The problem is not the school's making. The problem is a model for learning and, in particular, assessment, that can allow that such nonsense can be thought about, even for a second. As literate people, we all know that the more we read, the better we will, if we have to, write. More to the point, we all know that the 10-year-old who has enjoyed Philip Pullman's *His Dark Materials* trilogy will write better – more vividly, more flexibly, more *readably* and with better punctuation and grammar – than one who has read only reading-scheme books.

I have written about children writing so many times (see booklist for a few examples still in print) that all I want to say here is that, as children write, they learn about four things: themselves; their environment, natural, artificial, human, historical; their relationships with that environment; and their language. Therefore, they need frequent, highly charged opportunities to write with a purpose.

NOTES

I am a writer, obviously, or I would not be tapping away here. But before that, and senior to that, I am (and am proud to be) a teacher. Thus I use the pronoun 'we' freely. I think, as I tap, of my teaching in the past, in the present, and tomorrow, when I'll be in a school. I am constantly thinking about my own practice, and about what I see (and share in) other teachers' practice.

I anticipate one criticism of this book: that it not so much about literacy, as about creativity in language. That this criticism might even be thought of says something disturbing about the educational climate. All language activity, from thinking about what to cook for dinner, to writing a novel, a play or a poem, is at least potentially creative. And all teaching of language that isn't in some way creative will, though it may achieve short-term objectives, fail ultimately in the aim which all education has: in Lawrence Stenhouse's words 'to make us freer and more creative' (*An Introduction to Curriculum Research and Development* 1975).

Foundation Stage

How do they know the universe was made in a big bang, when there weren't any scientists around, not even dinosaur scientists?

My son, aged 5

The children are about to spend most of their waking hours away from their families, and now they meet these new and strange people: you and me. 'Foundation stage' rightly emphasizes both that experience, and also the importance of the teachers and LSAs who have chosen to teach the youngest children. So far so good.

But, unfortunately, 'foundation stage' suggests that those weeks provide a grounding for all learning; that they come to school with (as a teacher once put it to me) 'nil on entry'; that, to put it bluntly, their families have taught them nothing.

A moment's thinking will teach us that the foundations of learning, as distinct from schooling, have been laid years before the children come to school. Children arrive on that first day with learning gained, first, through their own innate curiosity; second, through their parents and other relatives; and finally, through their interactions with their natural as well as artificial environments. If we teach them as though that learning has not taken root, we damage them, insult their families, neglect their environment, and hazard many of their future learning chances. It is our job to help them to interpret the world, including, of course, the world of words – what the title of this book, bowing to current orthodoxy, calls 'literacy' – in the light of what they already know; which is a lot.

Everything we do should imply that we recognize this truth. Let's have no disrespectful names: 'littlies', 'babies' and the like. The staff at one prep school I know refers to the children in the pre-prep department as 'inkies'. When I ask why, it was explained to me that they were being incubated. Had no one thought this metaphor through? The children weren't even born – they were still eggs!

Before the children arrive on that first worrying, exciting day, one teacher fills the classroom boldly with things that they can, in all likelihood, already read.

Classrooms display should copy the style of a red-top tabloid front page: as Peter Dixon has pointed out in his book *Display in the Primary School*, the layout of the Sun has much to teach us about catching the eye.

Put up on the wall readable things like the McDonalds 'M' (this might cover a wall!), the Toys 'R' us shop sign, and the names, badges and colours of the local football team with other prominent national teams arranged around it. So some of these are 'only signs'? But words are 'only' signs.

The teacher does nothing about this display on that first day until story or poem time. The children will have spent the day, after all, playing, running, exercising in other ways, making new friends (and thereby, of course, learning about their language as they talk to and listen). Then she asks the children, 'Look around you. What can you read?' Many of them have come to her already telling her what they can read – because the display is so strong that it has caught the children's attention on and off all day.

Soon, this teacher brings the reading in the last idea down – or, rather, lifts it up – to the personal. At this stage in their schooling, it is important that the children's environment should be frequently changing. She takes down the logos, and replaces them with the words 'Mum' and 'Dad', in many different typefaces, and in handwriting, displayed under pictures and previously acquired pictures of the children themselves, with captions: 'This is ___'; or sometimes, 'Is this ___?'

I know that many children will, tragically, not find these words as positively resonant as other children will. This should not be used as a reason to discard these central words as tools for literacy or, more important, as tools for early thinking about love. 'This would be copping out' says this teacher. Make sure that 'Auntie' and 'Uncle' are prominent too, as well as 'Nanny' and 'Granddad'. Ask the children for other names given to people who look after them.

The teacher points to some part of the display, and asks the children: 'What does that say?' As soon as possible, she encourages children to write their own captions to these and other photographs. She praises all children's attempts. She tries to sow the seed of a culture in the school in which everybody is seen as, and they behave as, a writer.

Reading and listening to a story should not only be an end-of-the-day experience; it should be the substantive part of some lessons, too. A teacher is reading to children just after their morning break. The book is *Tiger in the Snow!* by Nick Butterworth. She doesn't go to the beginning of the story straight away. First she reads the blurb on the back cover. She is teaching the children about what a book is. She says to me later, 'I want to make sure that they know that a book can be as enticing as any new DVD'. She then holds the book up, showing its front cover. 'Can anyone tell me what this book is called?'. There is silence – but the children are gazing intently at the image, which is vibrant, unlike the cover of any reading book I – or they – have ever seen. How can a drawing be so full of movement, so pleasure-giving, so exciting?

She leaves time. They need that time to *think*. But still, there is no response.

'What's this?' she asks, pointing at the white stuff falling around the tabby kitten. 'Snow!' the children respond. 'And this says', she says, pointing at the words, *Tiger in the Snow*. Where do you think it says 'snow'? Can anyone come up and point?'

And someone does point, tentatively, at the right word: reads it.

And only now does she open the book, slowly leafing past the title page with its repetition of the title, the key phrase. By now the children are visibly impatient and thinking hard. What will happen next? She bends the book back so they can see the picture of the kitten, sad now, on the first page proper of the story. She hardly needs to read the words: she recites them, keeping her eyes on the children, mostly, rather than Butterworth's text.

The next page tells us that 'No one wants to come out to play'. She stops. Puts the book down. 'Has anyone found that? That no one wants to some out to play?' There is barrage of responses. 'Stop!' she says, quite fiercely. 'THINK about some time when you knew that no one wanted to come to play'. And the children tell her stories.

That was merely the cover, the title page and page one of a picture book. What have the children been thinking about? I count words, snow, books and friendship. And they are discovering, or re-discovering, how much pleasure is to be had from hearing someone read, or recite, exciting words. Almost enough to rival unpacking and slotting in a new DVD . . .

I use this book as an example. I could have chosen a book among literally hundreds: one of the best things that's happened to classrooms over the past two or three decades is the explosion in numbers and quality of picture books.

This is an idea for our own learning, and, perhaps, a colleague's. And that learning will enhance our ability to help the children's learning.

There is a kind of snobbery about picture books. Many of us have probably never felt the need to study one, to see how it works, and thence to become even more involved in it. Study *Tiger in the Snow!*. It is lively, rhythmic. It jumps and slides as its characters do. But beyond that, it breaks rules:

– It uses words that are not normally used in reading books on the grounds that they are too long, or multi-syllabic, or not open to conventional phonic analysis. 'Usually', for example; 'buried'; 'passengers'; 'unloads'.
– It uses sentences without main verbs: 'Usually.' 'A sledge!'; and 'Suddenly, WHOOOOOOOSH!'. It begins one with a connective: 'And doesn't stop . . .'
– It uses repetition, but not in the banal way that reading books do. 'Unusual' appears in various forms five times.
– It is not explicit: no 'ironing board' is mentioned in the text. In other words, like a 'real' novel, it leaves space for the reader's and the listener's thoughts and feelings. And is the kitten a cat or – a tiger?

'She reads the blurb on the back cover'. 'She leaves time'. 'They need to think.' Notice how the experience that the teacher provides for the children is like our own experience of reading a novel. Don't we read the blurb, turn the things over, examine it before we buy or even borrow a book?

This a central rule: all children's language experiences in the classroom, whether thinking, talking, listening, reading or writing, should be as much like the experiences we have as possible.

Assuming, of course, that we *are* readers.

I have done this many times with *Where the Wild Things Are* by Maurice Sendak, all the Judith Kerr *Mog* stories (e.g. *Mog the Forgetful Cat*) and dozens of others. These books remind me constantly that reading is supposed to make us think; and to help us feel. There is no such thing as a children's book. Any good book is simply a good book. Analyse, alone or, better still, with a colleague, one of these books.

Following on from Idea 4, this is another idea for our own learning.

On courses, I have often persuaded (with little trouble) teachers to share stories with each other. Most of us do this when we tell each other jokes, assuming we are the kind of person that can remember them, or when we share with a partner or a spouse what has happened at work during the day. Memories from early family life are stories we often tell, as well. But we can take this a step further, and talk to each other about a story that involves and entrances us: a novel, a television play, a story in a painting.

Talk about a novel film or TV programme that you love and, possibly, have admired from childhood, adolescence or early adulthood.

Then consider: what do our stories and children's stories have in common? I suggest, looking again at *Tiger in the Snow!*, *David Copperfield* (which I have just re-read) and an episode of *Fawlty-Towers* (which I have just re-viewed), that the connections are, among others: suspense, exploration of character, humour, and sheer joy in what language can do. Even more to the point, what do your responses have in common with theirs? We may show our reactions to, say, narrative suspense in different ways, but it is always there.

SHARE A STORY

I often bring in a soft toy that I have kept from my son's childhood. I tell the children a story about it. You must have many such stories about your own soft toys. Or your son or daughter (or grandson or granddaughter) must have told you theirs.

If the children bring in their favourite soft toys, I ask them: 'What are they called? Why did you call them that? What do they smell of?'. One 5-year-old said 'Babbit Rabbit smells [note, not "smelt"] of me, and only me'. 'When you are asleep, what do they get up to?'. Often children talk about mischief that they themselves might like to get up to, but don't, so Teddy does it instead. Bring in a vital word: 'Tell us a *story* about your teddy'.

Or some teddies protect their owners, and the children talk about love, affection, protection, even danger. This isn't 'just' literacy; it is powerful Personal and Social Education.

It is helpful if an adult – myself, an LSA, a parent – writes down some of the things they say. Then the lesson ends with a plenary almost entirely composed of the children's own words. The children listen and talk with attention and enthusiasm. They tell stories. And the stories should be kept for future reference (in a term's, or a year's time) when the children are more fluent in their reading. The store of anecdotes will have become a library book. It is worth printing a dozen copies for the classroom, and some for other people – the headteacher, for example. The book will have been (a word worth introducing early to children) published.

RHYME

Re-read *Tiger in the Snow!*

I read this book again, purely as a story first: it will bear a hundred re-tellings, as all good picture books do. But then I open out the pull-out page. I point to a group of words at the top of the page: 'bumping', 'humpy', 'jumping', 'lumpy'; then a group at the bottom: 'bouncing', 'prancing', 'dancing', 'rocking', 'rolling', 'twisting', and 'turning'. I get the children to say the words after me, running my hand along the print.

I point out the recurrence of '-ump', '-anc' and '-ing', and well as the alliteration (children are aware of alliteration years before they have to define it in Years 4 or 5). All this implicitly teaches the children that a good book works on different levels. This is more productive in the long term than the teaching of phonics: it teaches the importance of books; that they are not something that you read when you haven't anything else to do; that, as some one (Morrissey perhaps) sang, there may be more to life than a book, but not much more.

Later, in a PE lesson, I get the children to act some of these movements, as I silently hold out cards with the names printed on them, and then, if necessary, call them out. 'Jump', 'prance', 'dance', 'rock', 'roll', 'twist', 'turn'. I leave 'bump' and 'bounce' for a safer environment. During this lesson, I ask half the class to watch the other half as it moves. I ask them to look hard, to study their classmates, to watch the shapes they make with their arms and legs, the shapes they make as they move . . .

. . . So that, immediately after the PE lesson described above – before they're even changed, perhaps – I get the children to draw each other, in jumping, prancing, dancing, rocking, rolling, twisting and turning poses. I ask them to write, or dictate to an adult, the names of a child they have drawn and what s/he is doing.

I then produce the cards again, and we practise saying the words as playfully as we can.

RHYME – CONTINUED (BUT WITH ART)

There's a wonderful word! Notice how it ramifies in the language, leading to drama and theatre, to enjoyment, to sport, to music, all good things. Everything so far in this book – identifying logos, bringing in photographs, seeing them labelled, labelling them themselves, decoding those labels, listening to *Tiger in the Snow!*, thinking and talking about it, discussing their toys – all this is play. And play is what writers do. They play with words, and with what words can do. And everything that follows in this book is about play.

I mention this here, because the power of play in helping children (and everyone else) to learn has been blackened over the past 30 years. It has been mocked as trendy 60s nonsense and depicted as pointless. The media parrot the meaningless mantra that children should be doing 'real work' from day one in school; that the water tray and the sand tray that were fixtures in foundation stage classes until recently represented a decadent past; that playtime is now over, except for the parts of the day that the Americans call 'recess'.

But play and 'real work' are the same thing. The eyes of a child building with Lego; the eyes of an artist who makes objects from scrap metal; the eyes of a writer concentrating on her notebook or his screen (as I am now); the eyes of a scientist staring down a microscope; all these eyes have the same look of concentration, of total involvement.

And what connects them is the word 'learning'. As Freud wrote, 'The creative writer does the same thing as the child at play' ('Creative Writers and Day-Dreaming', quoted in Vernon [1970])

Why do some teachers think it is fair, let alone educational, to leave displays around for weeks, even terms? Those brand names and family names will have spent their usefulness quickly, at least for a time, so I store them away. I keep them, though: they'll come in useful later in the term, though not as useful as their cuddly toy anecdotes (see Idea 6 above). I put other images around the room that are central to their own lives.

Above all, I use their own artwork: paintings, drawings, models. They will have made many of these things in school with me, other teachers and LSAs.

But I also use other objects from their lives: Photos, souvenirs . . . objects that represent lives that are largely secret from school, lives lived who knows where? At home? Where they go on holiday? Where they visit, as an original home, every year? As long as we display these objects boldly, and in a way that they can interact with them, they give children much to think and talk about.

I try to ensure that all the children are represented on the walls, with their names. I put labels on the words in all the languages spoken by the children: not just the token *tavola* for 'table', *chaise* for 'chair', *porte* for 'door' and the like. I try to make sure that all the children know that *fenster* and *fenetre* are, respectively, German and French for 'window'. I am not just taking these pains for the children with other languages, but for my deprived (in this area, anyway) uni-lingual children too. Children like me.

Some teachers and LSAs have a gift for making striking displays, and an easy facility with line, brushstroke and primary colours. It is unfortunate if they use these gifts, such as they are, to make their own displays. It's even worse if they leave them on the wall to the point where, when a visitor asks the children, disingenuously, 'Did you make that painting?' they reply, 'No, the last class did it'. And it defies belief when the teacher, unabashed, explains that he did that mural two years ago . . .

I calculate that he made that painting, with its garish colours, its gnashing monster teeth, its wild swaying fronds, its unlikely coral colours, its sub-Disney-esque clichés for (certainly not with) children who are now in their second or third year at secondary school. At first, making this display was showing off; it was also a lack of understanding about what and how classroom walls can teach children; later, it became a symptom of laziness and indifference.

If I get carried away here, it is because a 'dramatic' undersea scene has been on the wall of one classroom since I've began going to that school three years ago. That teacher might have made a passable stab at window-dressing in a down-at-heel department school in say, oh . . . Newcastle-under-Lyme? But it has nothing to do with education.

It comes from a Key Stage 2 classroom, but the point I am making is relevant here.

When we teach PE, we teach language. And when we teach science, we teach language.

Science first. One of the strengths of both science and language, as far as school is concerned, is that we can't teach one without teaching the other.

Here is some science – is it natural science or physics? – that I have seen taught, and then taught myself.

I bring into the classroom balloons that I have, the evening before, or better still, two evenings before, filled with water and frozen in the school kitchen's freezer.

I put them in the water tray and invite the children to feel them. I record the children's words. I find that I hardly need to say anything as they explore, using their eyes and their fingers, ice melting, rubber splitting, the cold on their fingers. I throw some questions in, of course: 'What is happening now?' 'What does that feel like?' These questions arise from what is happening in the water tray, and how it impacts on the children. But better ones arise from how the children respond. The planning of my science lesson has become secondary: the children have taken first place in the scheme of things.

The words flow. What immeasurable learning is going on! They flow with greater force as little conversations develop about what's happening. I try to catch as much of it in my notebook as I can – immeasurable as it is, I want to get some frail grip on it. Then I read the children's own words back to them. The 'literacy' goes on. I type the children's words up; I publish them; I use them as a reading book; I show them off in front of the children to any sympathetic soul who will listen.

The children are cooking. My Year 6 correspondent sent me this recollection:

> In reception the whole class made soup. There were about 8 adults and the children were in groups of 4. One group did the cutting (we had to use plastic knives), another did the stirring (we used wooden spoons), and another did the adding, and another did the serving.

When I spoke to my correspondent, it turned out that the soup had been vegetable soup. The children had chopped onions, potatoes, carrots, celery and courgettes. The point here is the variety, not only of the vegetables or the tools, but of the words they used, especially nouns and verbs.

If I taught this lesson now, I would follow it up with a brief formal lesson on those words. As they would now have a context, the children would have an extra impulse to spell them conventionally. That word 'context' is critical in this work, as it is in the next two sections, as it is in all teaching of literacy. Note that 'phonemes', alphabets, punctuation pyramids and the like have no relationship to the lives children live.

In PE lessons, our words have a new resonance because they are about safety. The instructions, spoken in a more than usually serious tone, must be listened to, so that the children may not get hurt.

Eight used words from PE lessons. They were all verbs. Here come the nouns and adjectives, and not in the meaningless context of an alphabet round the room, but in the context of life, and life being experienced in an intense, because physical, way. I introduce new nouns: 'lungs' when they take deep breaths, 'heart' when they have run for a few minutes and can feel their quickened pulses, 'balance' as they sustain a pose on legs, bottom, or legs and arms. Then come familiar adjectives, like 'high' and 'low'; 'fast' and 'slow'; 'balancing/balanced' and 'falling'. They take on a sharper meaning in a new context.

On another day, I talk about these words, 'legs', 'arms', 'lungs' and 'heart', and their meanings. I ask the children to stand and place their hands on their legs and arms; then on where they think their lungs and heart are. There's often some useful discussion here. If I have multi-lingual children with me, I ask them to call out the words for their legs and arms, and then for their lungs and heart. I ask the children to draw their bodies, and to put labels on these organs, in whatever languages they choose: more than one, if possible.

This is another idea for our own learning about children's language and the way we teach it. I once analysed, with someone's help, my talk with the children. There are many ways of doing this: the first is to record lessons. Less systematically (but no less usefully) you can ask a colleague to make notes about your talk.

Talk about what you have found out. Roughly, what proportion of the time are we talking? How many open-ended questions do we ask, requiring more than a hands-up and a one-word answer? How many children did not say a word?

You will almost certainly find that you talk more than they do. I certainly found that, and when I had learned this, I recorded a lesson again, and I found that I was only slightly less likely to talk more often than the children did. I was still talking far more often that the children. The improvement was marginal.

Can this be right? Giving ourselves more practice in talk when we are already experts, and they are still learning? Also, I was distressed to find that a surprisingly large number of my questions were about trivia and discipline. 'Please could you open that window?' and 'Why are you doing that, Sidney?' add little if anything to the learning that was the supposed reason for everyone's presence. And why did I want to know why Sidney was doing that? Will knowing why help anything?

Discuss with colleagues: how can we ask more questions that are open-ended? Questions that leave gaps during which they can think: when a child stumbles for an answer, she is *thinking*, she is *learning*.

BRING BACK THOSE BRAND NAMES

I want to see and (more importantly) I want the children to see how much more readily they can read the McDonalds M, the Coca-Cola cursive, and the other logos now. We then discuss their progress. It is always encouraging, both for them, and for me.

I write up words associated with those images, and see if they can read them: 'burger', 'fries', 'United', 'City', 'Town', 'Barbie'.

This follows the process of the previous idea. When the children look again at those photographs and the sentences underneath them, I want to see, and I want them to see, see how much more they can read.

I then bring in other family-associated words, like 'brother', 'sister', 'aunt', 'uncle', 'grandma' and 'grandpa'. I ask the children for the names their grandparents have, and add those to the increasingly rich mix: 'Nanny', of course; but names peculiar to certain families: 'London Grandma', for example, and 'Big Grandpa' and 'Little Grandpa'.

Most of us have done this. I make a blue display labelled prominently in blue. 'Here is a blue hat, a blue clipboard, a picture of a blue sky, a blue policeman's helmet, a blue . . .' If I can find something massive – as tall as the classroom – that is blue – so much the better. I ask the children to bring in other blue things.

I go through the display with the children. This is all conventional enough. And, of course, I do the same again with red and green and yellow. But . . .

... Apart from making a corner of the classroom dramatic and colourful, and thus engaging the children, another purpose of this idea is to see how much children (or anyone else, for that matter) actually looks anything more than cursorily at my displays.

I label the (very prominent – domineering, if possible) blue display with an equally domineering label saying: 'This is our red display'. I want to see if they notice. I find that someone spots the deliberate mistake quite early in the day, and the word goes round. The aim is to surprise, and thus engage, the children. I take time out with all the children to talk about it. I repeat with the other primary colours.

Teachers have said to me that this only confuses young children. Well, that confusion leads to talk, listening and thinking. And which of us are not confused at some point in our learning? Isn't confusion, quite often, a necessary part of the whole business? I remember when a girlfriend gave me my first driving lesson. I got the car moving, and was confused when I found I had to change gear while travelling. I still experience confusion while following a complicated recipe, or when reading a new book of poems for the first time.

RED? BLUE?

I do the same with big/small, smooth/sharp, rough/smooth, old/new and, after a while 'people made these things/nature made these things'.

It is imperative for me that these displays are bold; that they take up plenty of room; that they contain unusual as well as everyday objects; that they don't outstay their welcome.

Both these ideas fly in the face of current orthodoxy. Everything surrounding children is supposed to be there to reinforce conventional views of punctuation and grammar. I don't believe they work, even in their limited terms. But more importantly, they don't provoke thought and talk. And these ideas do.

We don't have to open our mouths to begin our teaching: we begin to teach the moment we appear in the classroom. The expression on our face sets the scene. At the supermarket checkout, my experience can be a cheerful one, on the one hand, when the cashier greets me with a smile, and, on the other, a doleful one, when she is moody. Children un(or sub)consciously note our moods, and their experience is affected by them in the same way.

What we wear makes a contribution, too. Bright strong colours give children something to think and talk about. I often wear badges: I especially like wearing my Fungus the Bogeyman badge (a spin-off from Raymond Brigg's comic book of that name), and children nearly always talk to me about it. What pleases me especially here is that the children and I like Fungus for the same reasons: his repulsiveness expressed not only in his features, but also the range of greens which convey so much about him. I find my shamrock badge and my silver ring with a large bloodstone, bought in a souk in Dubai, leads to conversation with young children at lunchtime.

This casual talk is literacy at work – contextualized, meaningful and with a purpose.

The children at this nursery have only been in their large primary school half a term. Now, they and the staff spill untidily out of the nursery. All the staff, as well as a few parents, carry notebooks and pens. The children are mildly excited: they have only been out of their room as far as the playground on one side and the assembly hall on the other. Now they are going, the teacher has told them, on a journey.

At each stopping point – classrooms, stock cupboards, the boiler house that hums so interestingly – the adults ask the children questions, and prompt through and talk in other ways: 'What are the children in the hall doing? What's Mr ___ doing in here? Tell me some of the things that you can see over there. What can you hear?' The scene in the PE hall interests the children especially: four Year 6 children sway at the tops of ropes, others jump boxes, others balance in strange shapes, others swing hoops round their waists.

The nursery children gaze at the scene, and, as they drift away, they talk and the adults write their words down.

They arrive at the headteacher's room. He, of course, has been primed. He is standing on a chair polishing a high window, and stops theatrically, cloth in hand. He looks at the 25 children in his little office for a few seconds, then jumps down and greets them all by name. They ask him what he was doing . . . The teacher and the adults write down as much as they can of the children's questions, both now and outside in the corridor. The children chatter as the tour continues . . .

One of the parents types up the children's words, and prints a few copies. Later in the nursery, copies of 'Our Class Poem about Our School' are handed out to parents: 'Please can you read this to the children before they go to bed?' ask the teacher and the nursery nurse, explaining why.

It is a windy, rainy day. The same reception children are gathered at the window, watching trees bend, and an umbrella turns inside out as a woman struggles to make progress along the pavement.

The teacher turns the children's attention one by one to the leaden, tumbling sky, to the furiously swaying trees, to the people, to the umbrella. 'What does that look like?' 'What do you think it feels like, to be that lady over there?' 'Listen! What does everything sound like? Look at the road. Tell us about what the water looks like, what is it doing? Look at the water on the windows . . . '

Once again, the nursery nurse, the parents and others are writing notes, and they will later be typed up, published and displayed. But by now, many of the children are able to make their own notes. The adults praise every piece of writing, especially where a child has attempted a long, or a non-phonetically-friendly, word. Even some of the children who, in some schools' parlance, 'can't write yet' make marks that the adults interpret with the children's help.

ANOTHER CLASS POEM

How can we make displays that draw the children into them? How can we make the displays more than static decoration? Those McDonald images have long been put away. What should be arranged in the classroom?

First, I use postcard reproductions gathered from art galleries. Even the most modern art attracts and engages children's attention, while many, if not most, adults dismiss it irritably. Even these little images are resources, and I carry with me some hundred or so.

But large reproductions are even better. Van Gogh's 'Vincent's Chair' is in the Tate Gallery in London. I pin a large copy of the picture to a wall, and ask the children to look at the picture for some time. I ask them: What would this chair feel like to sit on?. What are the colours you can see in this picture?. What is the floor made of? Look hard at it. What are those marks (pointing at the brushstrokes)? How were they made?

All answers are valid. It doesn't matter that the children don't know about pipes: their speculation is part of their learning about language.

Don't tell the children about the artist's ear.
See – (clichés between Section 2: Key Stage 1 and Section 3: Key Stage 2)

I am looking at a reproduction of Gill's work, and I note these questions. They would apply, however, to any mother and child image: those by Henry Moore, for example, and the many hundreds of reproductions easily available in cheap but still elegant books available in remainder shops up and down the country.

What is she looking at? And Why?
What are her hands doing? Her right? Her left?
What is this image made of? (Is it paint? Stone?)

Can you think for a moment, and then tell me what is going on in the woman's head? And what is going on the child's head?

Do you remember sitting on someone's knee, someone who loves you? What do you feel? What do you think the grown-up feels?

ANOTHER IMAGE: 'MOTHER AND CHILD' BY ERIC GILL

OTHER OBJECTS FOR DISPLAY

I try to find objects that are interesting in themselves, that cry out to be handled, to be talked about: some are artistically interesting such as wooden carvings, especially carvings from other cultures than the Western European one, for example.

But many objects are to be picked off the ground, whether field, path, road or beach: stones, for example, which become interesting (if they aren't already) as soon as we get the children to reflect that they are infinitely older than they will ever be; shells; fossils; or found objects that have been disused, discarded and which are unnoticed. These are not interesting objects in the ordinary course of life for most people, but they assume an interest in the context of a classroom. And we want the children to become men and women (in Thomas Hardy's words) 'who notice such things'.

A shell's shape, for example: what lived in this? Where is the creature that lived in this now?

A discarded wagon wheel, for example, adds drama to the corner of a classroom, provokes words from the children, and is, of course an exemplar of a central concept in mathematics with all its related concepts (radius, circumference, diameter) which they are going to be familiar with in later years. Large plants, if only because they are still growing, always add something to a classroom.

These objects surprise by their very presence, and they suggest questions that cry out to be answered, if we think to ask them: What is this made of? How long do you think this has been in the road/field where I found it? What was this wheel for? Where have you seen other shapes like it?

This section applies to all stages.

In many towns there is an artist – more than one, probably – willing, eager even, to lend work to a local school: decent display of it, with which the artist will probably help, is good publicity. That artist may well agree to work with the children.

If the artist does that, we should remember two things: first, that the artist is not a teacher and, second that he or she is a teacher. Not a teacher in the sense that no professional qualification hangs at the end of his or her name; and he or she has no practice in basic teaching skills, such as gaining attention, imposing minor discipline etc; but is a teacher in the sense that no artist can work in front of us, and alongside us, without helping children and adults to learn.

In some schools, there will be anxiety about the safety of the pieces that the artist brings in. Will they get damaged? It is only in such schools that anything bad will happen. Trust the artist. Trust the children.

When the artist comes in, thinking, listening, talking and writing will follow as surely as fear follows the announcement of a coming Ofsted inspection, or as surely as a drop in morale follows the publication of league tables in the local press.

It is a kind of blasphemy to think of art in this way, as a means of teaching literacy. I feel uncomfortable writing these words. But among works of original work, more language is taught than under the dubious auspices of some reading scheme.

Key Stage 1

Once I was a little stream
But now I am a river
And soon I'll be the sea.
– Year 2 child's writing

Children do not morph into different versions of
themselves when they move from one stage of schooling
to another. They grow, and they grow at different rates
from each other, much as they have grown during each
stage. Hence, much of what I have written about the
Foundation Stage applies in Key Stage 1 (and also
applies in Key Stage 2). This is not just a matter of 'less
able' children growing more slowly. It is not even mainly
that. It is more that children need, throughout all their
schooling stages, time to think, time to talk, time not
only to listen but to be listened to. I have emphasized all
this in Foundation Stage. It is worth remembering that
they still have soft toys at home, and they still have much
to say about them; that they still need to play with
natural materials like ice and water, and with words; that
they still need to be surprised.

Apart from keeping out the weather, providing warmth and security, what are classrooms walls for? Haven't we, as a profession, been covering them with uninspiring display? In fact, so uninspiring that we are losing the critical ability to see for what it is!

For example, alphabets are arranged at 10 or 12 feet high around the room. The inaccessibility of these images to the children is only the first part of the problem. More importantly, they are usually made up of objects that have nothing to do with the children's lives: ducks for 'D' in an inner city school, for example; a big top man from a circus from about 1950 unconvincingly imitating the letter 'K'; . . . And, connected with both their inaccessibility and their remoteness from children's experience, they are, for the most part, ignored. They are a waste of space. Putting them up was a waste of someone's time and a waste of someone's professional ability. If there were a way of researching the attention children pay to this document, compared to the attention they pay to a cobweb high in a corridor on the way to assembly, the cobweb would win.

What should be there? What would enhance children's learning, and their confidence? Much of this part of my book is concerned with this. That tired old word primary school word 'Display' holds more questions inside it than many of us think.

I am very fond of these rhymes, and it is difficult to do this activity if you don't see some charm in them.

I recite to the children some traditional playground rhymes. This category tends to merge into another one, nursery rhymes, but that term smells so strongly of Edwardian middle-class households, with nannies, servants, and Mother and Father having as little to do with their children as possible, that I am surprised that it hasn't fallen completely out of use. Even so, there will be 'nursery rhymes' that are helpful with this work; thousands of them, in fact, in a book complied by the Iona and Peter Opie (see bibliography).

The first group of rhymes will be the ones that you and a colleague remember from your childhood. One middle-aged teacher had her class open-mouthed as she recited and did the actions to

Teddy Bear, Teddy Bear, turn around
Teddy Bear, Teddy Bear, touch the ground
Teddy Bear, Teddy Bear, go upstairs
Teddy Bear, Teddy Bear, say your prayers
Teddy Bear, Teddy Bear, switch off the light
Teddy Bear, Teddy Bear, say Goodnight.

I ask the children if they know any rhymes like these. Their contributions will make the second group.

Then often, for the third group, I have asked the parents when they call at the end of the day if they would write down rhymes that they remember from childhood.

Management theory often talks about the wider community, and involving it in the school. This all too often means grand schemes that require plans and (oh no, not another one) meetings. This exercise, on the other hand, starts at the bottom, and grows from its roots, like a tree.

Over the next few weeks, I try to spread the project more widely: carers, grandparents, colleagues, governors, local religious leaders, shopkeepers, the crossing patrol. For a secondary source, I go to The Opies' book (see bibliography).

I collect the rhymes. I read them frequently to the children. I print ten copies and leave them lying about. I lead an assembly with your children about them. I cover the walls with them: they are, after all, obedient, for the most part, to phonetic rules. I say them in lighter moments with the children. I ask the children to illustrate them.

I point out to the children that, in the title of these sections, 'ee' always makes the same sound; that 'gg' always makes the same sound, as does 'n'.

Preserve these rhymes. They will come in useful at Key Stage 2.

BRING BACK THE ICE BALLOONS

This is a winter lesson, and a lesson for a time when it is so cold that there has been freezing overnight. It is also a lesson (as are several in this book) that point up the continuity between stages: it is necessary to keep in touch with what other teachers have done with the children you teach now.

I pick up the lesson I taught with a colleague in the Foundation Stage about the ice balloons. I read to the children the words that they said, and which I or a colleague had written down. I repeat the experiment.

I ask the children to look up 'ice' in all available books; to google 'iceberg', 'icecap'; to collect as many ice words as possible. If there is ice outside, I talk with them about safety. I ask the children for similes for ice.

I discuss with them scientific ideas:

What was ice before it was ice?
What made it change?
What will the ice change into soon?
Why will that change occur?

Cookery is always the application of science. This is a comfort to those of us who enjoy making dinner, but who consider ourselves scientifically near-illiterate. Cookery is also the application of words. So children cooking are learning both science and literacy.

I asked my Year 6 correspondent about cookery lessons that she remembered, and she wrote to me about a lesson she remembered from Key Stage 1:

> We made pancakes. One group went to the shops to get the ingredients, another put the ingredients into the separate bowls, another made the pancake mix, Miss cooked them and when they cooled down everyone had a go to flip them and we ate them with a scoop of ice-cream.

Imagine all the language going on here: on the way to the shops and words about safety and traffic; the discussion about the ingredients, and the luscious words as they ate.

SCIENCE, COOKING AND MORE WORDS

There exists a writing scheme that tells teachers to insist that children must change colour pens while writing. They must write with a blue pen. Whenever they need a full stop, they must put that blue pen down, and pick up a red one, and use that for the full stop. Whenever they need a capital letter (immediately after a full stop, of course), they must put down their red pen, and pick up use a green pen for the capital (that they will have started with, of course). Then they must reach for the blue they used to begin with, after the green, of course.

Think how that must have deflected the children from the task of writing; of putting meaningful sentences together. The first time I saw this in operation, I saw that the Year 2 class had lost all the attack and the fluency which I had observed in the same class a year before when they were a year younger, and most of the interest they had in their subject, as they fiddled about with poor quality felt tip markers, the sort that make hairy marks on paper.

Note now that 'tells', 'insist' and 'must' in that first paragraph. As the art educator Robin Tanner pointed out, all art involves choice, which involves discrimination, which is an indispensable condition of learning. These children were having choice, even in the least important matters, taken away from them.

FADS: SPELLING

There are schemes that reduce literacy to spelling.

'Literacy' was invented as a back formation* of 'illiteracy', and first used in 1883. It represented a need (among other things) to fill offices with young working class people who could read and write. Conventional spelling was then vital. It is less important now, and will become even less important as computers, with their spell checks, become even more ubiquitous.

It is a mistake to talk of 'correct' spelling: there is only 'conventional' spelling, and that concept is only as old as Johnson's Dictionary (1775). Even today, it is legitimate to spell 'judgment' like that or as 'judgement', and 'ageing' like that or without the 'e'. The '-ize' ending in words like 'customize' can be '-ise', and should we spell 'primeval' like that or in the way that nods in the direction of its Latin origin, 'primaeval'?

'English' and 'language' are both nobler words than literacy.

*a back formation is a word formed from a longer word.

There are schemes that reduce literacy to handwriting. It is unprofessional to impose a handwriting style on children for the reasons explained below.

Implementing such schemes – italic, cursive, whatever – takes up much time that could be spent teaching children to communicate, both with themselves, and with others. When a child in her notebook, or a teacher on her smart board, are wondering how to form the next letter in the prescribed manner (can anyone, by the way, handwrite well on a smart board, let alone in a prescribed manner?), neither she nor you is thinking about what needs to be said. A handwriting policy is, in other words, a means of control.

A scheme requires (and gets, in many schools) an unpleasant policing, when the children's books are watched by the imposer of the scheme.

It presents problems to a teacher who has learned to write legibly in a different style. If you were taught italic (as I was) or Nelson (as my son, a teacher) was, it is not easy to produce, say, cursive on the white board. And what does it do to your personal handwriting, which becomes an anonymous hybrid? The same applies to children moving from a (say) cursive-teaching school to an italic-teaching one. And then to an easy-going school that (merely!?) requires legibility? Do handwriting scheme proponents ever give any thought to changes in children's lives?

They are a curtailment of children's self-expression. They represent a reactionary and redundant requirement when most communication in the world of work will be done with computers.

I wrote about science in Ideas 13 and 14. One teacher I spoke to was aghast when I told her that all her cookery lessons were all chemistry lessons as well. But they are. And all cookery and all chemistry lessons are literacy lessons too because they all require words.

I wrote about PE and what it can help us teach in terms of language in Ideas 14 and 15.

Now the children are more mature and their language is more fluent. I ask them to think about their bodies again before most PE lessons, and about the words that we all use to talk about them. We spend some ten minutes or so talking and listening

Where I am allowed, I photograph them as they run, stretch, balance, jump, swirl a hoola-hoop, chase a ball, swing a rope. I show the photographs to the children, and ask them to write captions for them: 'Alice is jumping in this picture'; 'When I run, I feel as though . . .' (get them to finish sentences like this one); and so on.

Afterwards, I talk about these words and their meaning. If I have the opportunity, I build all this material up into a wall display and a library book.

I will be writing about standing orders for writing at Ideas 71 to 75 in Section 3: Key Stage 2. All that applies here at Key Stage 1. The main point to make is that children can write. They need to be helped to understand this from the very beginning. Build on the fact that they scribbled on the walls when they were three; they were announcing their existence by doing so. They were writing. They need opportunities to write everyday, with their materials – pencil and paper – always near at hand.

There are two keys to teaching poetry writing in school.
They apply especially to children in Key Stage 1.

The first is that children enjoy rhythm, rhyme, pattern
and surprising juxtapositions of words and sounds.
We know this from the first time we dandle a baby on a
leg and chant:

> Ride a cock-horse to Banbury Cross
> To see a fine lady on a white horse
> Rings on her fingers and bells on her toes
> And she shall have music wherever she goes.

It simply does not matter that the child does not fully
understand these words: indeed, they are still, at least
partly, a mystery to me.

Because of this enjoyment, they are open to poetry,
with its bardic magic and its playfulness, and need to
have a daily helping of it.

The second key to teaching poetry to young children is
'structure'. All the poems we have read to them have a
clearly defined shape. The rhyme I've quoted above, for
example, is made up of two rhyming couplets; though the
first rhyme pair, 'Cross / horse' is actually a half-rhyme,
reflecting, possibly, a regional pronunciation of one of the
words.

We don't need to supply their subject matter. They
have that, and they have it in plenty – their lives, their
friendships, their troubles, their joys, their sadnesses,
their relations, their toys. And the facts that they have
had these experiences, and that they need to reflect on
them makes poetry central to their emotional education.
But they do not have the structures they need to express
their feelings about these things, or even to describe
them. Art, as Leonardo da Vinci writes somewhere, has
to be put in prison in order to be set free. The following
five ideas are little prison cells that set young writers free.

Poetry is a powerful medium for writing at Key Stage 1 for several reasons. The first is its unthreatening brevity. This lesson is an example.

Offer the children a sentence from your own life. For example, there's my (late, last Sunday) cat:

> I loved you
> Stanley
> Even though
> You used to kill birds.

Ask them to write little stanzas on this model. At first they will probably come up with stanzas like this:

> I love you
> Mum
> Even though
> You shout.

But we can widen, and enrich, the remit. It's not just people. There are objects too that we feel ambivalent about – weather ('Look out of the window!'), food, music – and the children are soon writing stanzas like this:

> I love you
> Sunshine
> Even though
> You fade away.

Notice how the structure, with the use of the sense of sight, has given this sentence an echo of something beyond its literal meaning. You wouldn't have got a little stanza like this by asking something like 'Can you write a verse about why sunlight can be sad?'! Whether we as adults are fully conscious of it or not, 'sunshine', in this child's writing, becomes somewhere in the back of their minds (and ours) a metaphor for something like 'happiness'

STRUCTURE: STANZAS FROM SENTENCES

Now is a good time to introduce the other senses ('those precious five', as the poet W. H. Auden calls them somewhere). Indeed, when this becomes part of the standing orders of a classroom when they children are writing, the quality of that writing shoots upwards.

Ask the children to think about the sense of smell:

I love you
Evie [a baby sister]
Even though
You stink.

Or hearing:

I love you
Violin
Even though
You are screechy.

I love you
My old dog Barny
Even though
You don't bark anymore.

Using the same structure, introduce the other senses: touch, taste.

I love you
Chips
Even though
You make me fat.

I love you
Jeremy's fur [a cat]
Even though
You hate it when I stroke you the wrong way.

The aim here is to set the children free from what might be called 'common sense', to help them to escape the ordinary. Ted Hughes puts this graphically when he writes: 'The progress of any writer is marked by those moments when he manages to outwit his own inner police system'. There is in all of us a nagging voice asking all the time 'Does this make sense? Can I really write that?' Children are less in thrall to this voice, but they sometimes need help to escape its tentacles.

I give the children this structure:

I don't like to boast
But . . .

The children have to add the most outlandish sentences. I find that some discussion about the word 'boast' is helpful. I introduce synonyms like 'brag' and 'show off'. Later with Key Stage 2, I would introduce the idiom 'blow my own trumpet' and even the French 'send flowers to myself'.

At first, though, their suggestions will be tame, as in 'I'm a good footballer' and 'I wear pretty dresses', and you laugh such stuff to scorn: 'Call that a boast?' They haven't escaped that inner copper, that nagging voice demanding common sense. I give them some of my own boasts, such as:

I don't like to boast
But
When I look at a clock, I can make time stand still.

and

I don't like to boast
But
Jamie Oliver asks me for advice on cooking pasta.

This livens the children's writing up.

Towards the end of one session, one child wrote:

I don't like to boast
But
I have a secret that I'm never going to tell
ANYONE!!!!!!!

Notice again that echo: the writing has developed during a few minutes' discussion and practice from the everyday to the humorous, to the personal, to a sentence that will evoke an emotional response in all the other children, and all the adults, in the room.

The next structure works with all ages, but you add complications, depending on how fluent you judge the children to be.

> I used to . . .
> But now I . . .

A nervous boy in Year 1 said once in his Suffolk accent (and we wrote it down quickly, and made a fuss of it):

> I used to be in my mum's belly.
> But now I am not.

A sophisticated Year 2 girl wrote:

> I used to be a Christian
> But now I'm an atheist.

And she later added, once I had introduced the idea of the future tense (see next idea):

> And soon I'll be a pagan.

I met her again in Year 6, and the school had preserved her writing. I didn't feel it would be right to ask about her religious position.

Later, I follow the same procedure as above, but introduce the future tense. This becomes PSME (Personal, Social and Moral Education) in a more intense way as the children write, in their little stanzas, about their past, their present and their future, and about their hopes and aims for the future. They review how their lives are progressing. They do this both in the act of writing, and in the act of reading their writing afterwards: to themselves silently, to a friend, to a teacher or an LSA, and eventually, perhaps, to the rest of the class. And if their work is published – 'made public' – by being displayed, or printed in a little magazine for parents, governors and inspectors, they rejoice more and more widely in their progress.

> I used to not be able to swim
> But now I can swim with arm bands
> And soon I will be able to swim without arm bands.

One child wrote:

> I used to be bad
> But now I am good
> And soon I will be an angel.

This led to heckling from the adults: 'But Chrissie, you've always been an angel!'

STRUCTURE: LOOKING AHEAD

I change, slightly, the structure above, and ask the children to think about other changes outside their own lives: in nature, for example, the weather, or the lives of animals; or in the lives of buildings. I offer a different sentence construction. The new version is: 'Once I was . . . But now I am . . . and soon I'll be . . .'

Some examples from a Year 2 class:

> Once I was a little stream
> But now I am a river
> And soon I'll be the sea.

> Once I was a cocoon
> But now I am a moth.

And, rather heartlessly,

> Once I was a piglet
> But now I am a pig
> And soon I'll be bacon.

Other structures include:

I know an angel who . . .

Or substitute 'devil', 'giant' or 'monster' in those beginnings. They all work here, too. This can be adapted to many a project.

I know a giant who is big, and helps me when I fall over.
I know a monster who lives in an empty house down our road.

Think up other structures along the same lines. Note that 'and' and 'but', tiny little conjunctions, or connectives, make a central difference to sentences. For example:

> For my dinner I had . . .
> But I would rather have had . . .

Yesterday, a student teacher suggested another structure:

> I must . . . [do something]
> Or . . . [this will happen].

I tried this the next day with children, and one wrote:

> I must go to the toilet
> Or I will wet myself.

Later, the children and I widened the remit with different pronouns, such as 'you', 'we' and 'they':

> You must stop when I blow the whistle
> Or I will be angry.

Once again, among all this creative writing, grammatical terms are present: 'connective', 'pronoun' etc. Children, like us, become more literate as they listen, talk and write.

DRAWING AND LITERACY

You will have noticed how quiet children go when they are asked to look at some object 'until' (as William Blake puts it somewhere) 'it hurts'; and then to draw it. This quietness, brought about by close observational drawing, is evidence of how intense their thinking is when they look, and use a pencil to try to record what they are looking at.

Drawing calms them. It sensitises them, first, to what they are studying, and, second, to what they feel about it. It enables them to concentrate in a way that simply looking, however hard, can't. I have recently discovered for myself the pleasure of photographing architectural details, and composing a shot has a similar (thought not nearly so intense) an effect.

There is a relationship, mysterious it may well be, between a child's fluency with the line she uses when she is draws, and the line she uses when she writes: the fluency achieved while drawing feeds into the writing. And indeed, vice versa. Either way, every line, to use a phrase from the artist Paul Klee, is a line into knowledge. I wrote a book (2002) with the title *Lines into Knowledge*, but the publisher wouldn't let me use it. The book was eventually called *Enabling Children's Learning through Drawing*. For present purposes, it could be called *Enabling Children's Literacy through Drawing*.

Do we offer children enough chances to draw, bearing this connection in mind?

CLOSE OBSERVATIONAL DRAWING

This has been a standby for progressive teachers since the late sixties. But, cliché as it might seem, it provokes thinking. Therefore it has power, power for teaching, not only about lines used in drawing, but also about the right words for the situation.

See Leonardo's sketchbooks, for example.* He wrote above, below, between and around his drawings. It looks as though he couldn't draw without writing, and as though he couldn't write without drawing. And while he was doing both, he was thinking. About words.

I present the children with everyday objects: shoes, boots, plants, faces, their own hands, bits of car engines. Some of these objects might be things seen conventionally as beautiful – flowers, for example – but most are everyday things, because there is beauty in a boot, say, with its laces trailing, a trowel, a spade, a garden fork, tools of 'all trades, their gear and tackle and trim' – when they are observed with attention, and recorded in drawing. This is because they are associated in our minds with the human beings who wore or used them.

I ask the children to draw them following the four rules of drawing:

> Don't use erasers. I tell the children to leave their 'wrong' lines where they are, and to then draw the 'right' lines in a way to show their importance. This helps to devalue the photographic fallacy – that all drawing aims at the depiction of physical reality – and is the practice of many artists.
>
> Keep on looking. I ask the children to concentrate on just two things: the movement of the point of the graphic tool – pencil, charcoal, whatever – and the object they are recording.
>
> Use your pencil in as many ways as possible. I often give the children small rectangles of paper before the drawing begins, and ask them to fill them 'with as

many different marks as possible', and to use those
marks in their drawings

Draw it close up: This helps the children to draw
larger than they sometimes do, in order to include
details.

Half way through the lesson, I suggest that the children
might write words, phrases or sentences on their
drawings, describing what they are looking at.

Later, I ask them to move around the room, looking at
each other's work, and thinking of things to say that are
both kind and true (or not unkind, and not untrue) about
each other's drawings.

*Three examples are *Leonardo da Vinci: The Anatomy
of Man* by Martin Clayton, *The Drawings of Leonardo da
Vinci* by A. E. Popham and *Leonardo's Inventions* by Jean
Mathe, trans. David MacRae.

DRAWING: CAPTURING THEIR MOOD

I ask the children to draw 'the insides of their minds' when they are angry. While to many adults this may sound obscure, even pretentious, all children in my experience understand what I asking them to make: abstract drawings that capture a mood, not representational drawings. They are drawing their anger.

I ask them: What kind of lines will you need to make with your pencil (or charcoal or whatever)?

If they are using colour – though I think it best to use black pencils at first for this exercise – what colours best suggest anger?

As they draw, I ask them what feelings are filling their minds, what's going on in them, and to write words, phrases or, sometimes – quite often at this stage – sentences, where they think best on the paper.

Then, of course, I ask them to read what they have written, and show what they have drawn, to other children. Some of the children will have had their words scribed, of course, and some will have not written fluently: these children will read what they can, and someone will help them read the rest.

And then I have the raw material for another book for the class library.

I ask the children to draw things that most people would not seem worth drawing. For example, I take them into the hall, and ask them to draw the climbing frame, and to think (first) then talk (second) and then (last) write about three things as they draw:

What does the frame look like from where you are?

What memories do you have of being on the frame?

What do you see when you are on top of the frame?

All the while, as they draw, think, talk and write, they will be developing their literacy skills.

DRAWING: DEVELOPING LITERACY SKILLS

DISPLAY AND LITERACY

I have often noticed, with some sadness, that children hardly ever look at displays. When I was a young teacher, I used to spend hours every week (hours that, were I a young teacher today, I would have to spend filling in forms and writing reports) carefully arranging their work on my classroom walls; but they hardly ever noticed my handiwork, which was, after all, intended to show off theirs. Well, on the face of it that was the purpose. I wonder sometimes now whether I was just showing off. The phrase 'ego-trip' was then unheard of.

What can we do to displays to draw the children to them? How can we make the displays more than static decoration, so that they contribute to their learning and, in particular, to their development in literacy?

I use:

Objects that cry out to be handled: wooden carvings, especially carvings from other cultures than the Western European one; stones; large plants

Images that surprise and arrest, cut from magazines, perhaps, and discarded as soon as their impact has lessened

Displays that surprise (like the blue/red displays I mentioned in Key Stage 1)

And above all, I display the drawings, with the writing, done in the previous lessons.

Surprise is an under-rated way of drawing attention to something you want the children to learn.

I put something unusual in front of each group of five or six children. The examples I give below are randomly chosen from what I can see as I sit writing this, and what I remember doing in the past:

An African carving of a young woman's head

A huge houseplant

My grown-up son's first baby shoe

I zoom round the classroom, asking each group some questions:

What do each of you think the woman in this carving is thinking? Look at her face. Her eyes.

Can you describe the shapes and colours in this plant?

This boot: tell me about the man or the woman who has been wearing it. Make up a story all about the adventures this person has had today. You could tell the stories from the boot's point of view.

And, of course, before they're talking, and while they're talking, and after they have talked, they will be thinking.

I write down some of the things they say, and other colleagues in the room help me. Then the lesson ends with a plenary almost entirely composed of the children's own words. Again, they are learning (to put it in the modern way) listening, thinking and reading 'skills'.

REPRISE

I suggest that teachers bring back those images they read
when they were in Foundation Stage; the McDonalds M,
the Coca-Cola cursive, the Toy 'R' Us shop sign, the
brand name of cars, the names, badges and colours of the
local football team and so on.

I suggest that teachers ask: how many of these can you
read? It is time for the children to congratulate
themselves on how much stronger their grasp of words is
now, compared to what it what a few months ago.

Almost all children have been surrounded aurally by rhyme all their lives. They may have heard it in nursery rhymes, like 'Ride a cock horse'; but even if the notion that children no longer hear these rhymes is true, they have certainly heard other rhymes in advertisement jingles and television programmes, and in songs. Some parents sing to them as games or lullabies, and their older siblings sing in the pop songs. Finally, they may (the lucky ones) have heard rhymes in poetry.

I read a great deal of poetry to children, and am always struck by how receptive they are to it in a way that nearly all adults aren't. I read this poem of my own for the pleasure I hope it gives, and then I point out the rhymes.

Long time ago

There were dragons, there were unicorns
  That slid in the snow.
There were fairies in forests
  Long time ago.

There were mermaids and mermen
  And for all I know
There was a golden gryphon
  Long time ago.

There was a purple penguin
  And a crimson crow
With rubies for eyes . . .
  Long time ago. (Fred Sedgwick)

The spelling relationships between them: 'snow' . . . 'ago' . . . 'know' . . . 'crow' . . . well, there's plenty of literacy there. If we feel like following the finicky inanities of the Literacy Strategy, we might point out the 'onsets' – 'g', '[k]n', 'cr', and the rimes 'o' and 'ow'. We might collect other examples from the children: 'blow', 'flow', 'no', 'show' and so on. We might then complicate matters with some of the children – and put a small firecracker under the bottom of the phonics argument – by bringing up 'though'. And 'how' and 'now'.

I say this rhyme to children:

I'll tell you a story
About Jack-a-Nory,
And now my story's begun.

I'll tell you another
Of Jack and his brother
And now my story is done.

With my eye on phonics, I ask the children to look at
'story . . . Nory', 'begun . . . done' , and 'another . . .
brother'.

Using books by the Opies, I find other rhymes, and ask
the children to identify pairs of rhymes. I ask them, in
groups, to distinguish between rhymes that use the same
letters ('coo', 'moo') and others that use different letters
('do', 'through', 'Timbuktu').

And I follow the same procedure with this one:

Georgie Porgy, pudding and pie,
Kissed the girls and made them cry.
When the boys came out to play
Georgie Porgy ran away.

Or this:

Deep deep down in Stratford Town
A pretty girl puts on her gown.
She runs in the road, she runs in the meadow
But all the boys can see is her shadow.

She runs by the road near tall St John's,
She runs where the cricketers play.
She runs so fast in her green-gold gown
And the pretty girl runs away, away,

The pretty girl runs away.

She runs in the roads, she runs in the meadow
But all the boys can see is her shadow.

All the boys can see is her shadow. (Fred Sedgwick)

One sure way to help children to understand the point and purpose of writing is to set up a correspondence for them. This could be with children in a local school, or better in a school in another part of the country, or even better, another country; it might be a correspondence with an adult in the community who is ready to set an hour or two aside once a week or so to read their letters and reply to them: priest, imam, crossing patrol lady or gentleman, someone in the local baker's . . .

A plea against stereotypes!

This applies throughout this book, in all stages. So I have put it somewhere in the middle. Let us beware of clichés:

Van Gogh is infinitely more than the sad story of his ear.

Henry VIII's wives matter far less to the history of England than his tyranny and his break with Rome.

Tutankhamen and his ubiquitous mask are largely irrelevant to Ancient Egyptian history.

Poetry for children is more than light verse (though some light verse such as Allan Ahlberg's verses and all books by the American Shel Silverstein are very good). Any book with 'pimple', 'bogey', 'underpants' or 'knickers' on the cover is to be distrusted.

Bangladesh is far, far more than flooded fields and disaster.

Paris is far, far more than the Eiffel Tower.

Suggested story openings, such as 'Once upon a time', 'In a country far, far away', 'It was a dark and stormy night' are not only clichés, but invitations to copy more clichés.

Key Stage 2

Neither Youth nor Childhood is Folly or Incapacity
William Blake in a letter written in 1799

Children do not change, as I have already written, into different versions of themselves between the end of one schooling stage and another. The danger here is that, because primary schooling is traditionally divided at this point between infant school and junior school, we might behave as though there has taken place, in the summer holidays, a great alteration. I worked in a junior school once where the children had been taught to read, in the infant school, using traditional orthography (these letters) and then, once they were between seven and eight years old, and if they were labelled 'slow readers', were taught using i.t.a. (the initial teaching alphabet). This was an alphabet that had some forty-odd characters, providing a one-to-one correspondence with the (supposed) number of sounds. It has sunk without trace.

That is an extreme example. But it is a shame if the children in Year 3 suddenly find that their book troughs disappear, to be replaced by duller shelving; to find a kind informality replaced by a strange straitlacedness; to find a cooler atmosphere than the one they have been used to.

I try to ensure as much continuity as I can between their experiences in infant classes, and their experiences in junior classes.

ALPHABETS PUNCTUATION PYRAMIDS

Let's reflect for a few moments on many phenomena that conventionally pass as aids to literacy, think about them – and then question them.

Alphabets arranged at ten or twelve feet high around the room: they are often still there at the beginning of Key Stage 2 (and often the same ones.) The inaccessibility of these letters to the children is only the first part of the problem. As I wrote earlier, it is more important to note that they are usually made up of images that have nothing to do with the children's lives. Children, with their usual critical acuity, ignore them.

The Punctuation Pyramid: I am looking at one now. When I ask teachers what it is for, I get different answers. Someone said that it was to show the order in which certain punctuation marks were to be taught. But why is this something to display to children? Once I saw it displayed, not as a pyramid, but as a saltire, the shape of St Andrew's cross, with the skinny bit in the middle. What is it for? Answers on a postcard, please.

Rows of dictionaries and thesauruses: These books are, obviously, vital tools in any classroom. But class sets of them? Is everybody at the same moment in need of such a book? Are you seriously ever teaching 'literacy' with the same tools to a class where some of the children are devouring the last book of Philip Pullman's *His Dark Materials* trilogy, and others still finding joy in less demanding texts?

Star charts. These would depress anyone concerned with children's self-esteem and fairness as much as anything in classrooms.

Oh look! Rachel, Marcus, Declan and Jeremy have so many stars for hard work and good behaviour that the most recent few have been crunched in on the right hand side and are spilling over the margin. On the other hand, Daniel, Georgia, Freddie and Cariad have not progressed beyond three or four stars. I notice tell-tale evidence that the last-named has had one star removed. I want to ask what crime led to this, but feel it wouldn't be good form. I find this girl and eye her for signs of delinquency.

I can think of few things that are such a demoralizing day-by-day reproach to some children, and a possible cause for gloating by others (though, to their credit, Rachel and her three friends seem to set little store by it).

A student teacher has just asked me, what would I put in their place? Why is there any need for external rewards? We have to understand as far as possible each child, and judge how we might make their performance better.

IDEA
64

A MEANINGFUL ALPHABET

An early exercise, also suitable for Key Stage 1, is to *commission* the children to make their own alphabet, with the promise that it will be *published* (I like to use those italicized words early with children, to make them part of the classroom discourse about language, as they are about professional writing).

I would point out that there should, perhaps, be two panels for 'G': one with a gun (why not, if someone has chosen that word?) or a goose or a garage for the hard 'G'; and one with a George or a Georgia (if there's one in the class) or a genie or a gem for the soft 'G'. Perhaps there should be panels for 'Ph' and 'Th' as well. They should decide.

The children might discuss where in the classroom it would be most useful. As a frieze? Where? Up there? Down there? As a published book, available for reference (five copies will be sufficient) alongside a couple of dictionaries, thesauruses and atlases?

They might make an alphabet that could be used at Foundation Stage and another for Key Stage 2. They could discuss what the difference between the two alphabets might be, and present their alphabets to the younger children.

This is hard to write about without stating the obvious: you need books of high quality around the children, and they have to be available all the time. But of course, this begs a question: 'What is a book of quality?'

A book of quality, at the very least, *raises questions in the reader's mind that are of significance to the reader's life:* about the reader's relations with himself, and her relationship with the world. Examples include: *Where the Wild Things Are* by Maurice Sendak, *David Copperfield*, The Q'uran, The Bible, all of Anne Fine's novels, and all of Michael Morpurgo's novels.

None of these lies dead on the shelf when we put it down: all of them go on living in our minds. To return to a recurrent theme in this book, they are books that make the reader (or the listener) *think*.

Children encounter books of low quality as they visit shops with their families especially at Christmas. Brand names. Pink for the girls, blue and red for the boys. Showy and vulgar. Stereotypical male and female images. Hannah Montana. Barbie books. Football books issued by individual clubs. These books raise no questions at all. They require no reflection. Their purpose is to sell more merchandise. Can a book of no quality teach literacy?

We might reflect, with a colleague, on books that we read that have involved us and even changes the way we thin k and feel?

We might learn much here from the display of books in Foundation Stage and Key Stage 1 classrooms. They use troughs as well as shelves, so that large books can be more readily looked at, picked out and read. With non-fiction, it is important that everything is up-to-date. It says much about a school where the atlases still show the USSR, Yugoslavia and Czechoslovakia.

I would throw out tired copies. The only dog-eared books worth keeping are those in the homes of collectors (often children) who can't bear to part with a book given in childhood by a loved and remembered grandparent, or a school prize.

I would reinstate the library. Of course children should become familiar with the internet, but, like public libraries, many school libraries are becoming second-class areas, neglected alongside computer suites with internet access. When I wanted to give away some art books because I was moving from a large house into a flat, not one secondary school in my town was interested. 'We are thinning out at the moment' said one teacher. And another: 'Our students Google'.

See Ideas 3 and 4 for what makes *Tiger in the Snow* a book of quality. Re-read, or if necessary, read it for the first time. The rhythms, the originality and the look of this book far transcend the fact that was written and illustrated with young children in mind. Also, it is healthy and enjoyable for children to remember the good times, when books like this were on the menu, at home and in school, everyday.

When I do this, I point out some of the grammar in the book: all those 'ing' words are present participles, for example, verbs describing something going on; I note that one-word sentences are (despite conventional teaching) powerful sometimes. I point out, too, the use of repetition.

I ask the children to make a poem called 'Tumbling through the snow'.

I ask the children to write and illustrate a picture book for a four-year-old. I ask them to think, first, of what such a book needs. I suggest simpler sentences than the ones they have become used to, vivid illustrations, humour–I ask them to think about what a four-year-old will find funny: what made them laugh when they were four or five years old, mystery–a surprise on the last page is always satisfying, both to think about and write, and, later, to read, repetition. This is not chiefly because it helps teach words (though it does) but mainly because children like it. It is reassuring, and is an important element in a prose rhythm.

I find that this activity is often best done in pairs. The conversations between children as they think about, talk about, write and illustrate their stories present powerful opportunities for learning. But note: the children should share both tasks, rather than assigning the writing to one and the illustrating to the other.

I suggest that there are more ways of illustrating than simply drawing: what about collages made up from magazines? I ask the children to think of other ways.

I ask the children to take the stories home to read to young children. Next day, I follow this up: 'How did it go? How can you make your stories better?' I try to fix a date with a Key Stage 1 class so that we can try the stories out on their intended audience.

Notwithstanding what I have written about good books, the main aim of the reading display is to show that reading is a much more varied activity than we often assume. Children who have experienced a block in their learning to read will often find that the book itself, as an object, discourages them. A footballer replied to a questionnaire sent by children in a middle school about favourite books 'I have only ever read one book, and that is *Charlie and the Chocolate Factory*, so I suppose that must be my favourite book'.

Blocked. By an engaging book. Sad.

I ask the children to name a few of the examples of texts that they read. They should cast the net as wide as possible, and beyond the obvious things like books, comics and newspapers. This does not run counter to my argument in Idea 63: it simply shows how we read often, almost without realizing it. What I read almost everyday includes cereal packets, captions in television ads, slogans in ads in other places, street signs, cartoon captions.

I ask them to collect from relatives examples of things that they remember reading, and to bring them in to school: not just books, but examples from the above list and other things I haven't thought of.

I discuss the display at various times over a few days. I pass the items around. Some will have to be handled carefully, of course, and that is part of the learning: the ration book and the letter will be precious. So is the collection of football programmes: otherwise, it wouldn't be a collection. While I distrust the stereotyping of boys as slower readers, I hover over them while some of less fluent read words in the football programmes, for example: 'striker', 'midfield', 'penalty area'.

One display is a classroom contained:

A handwritten note with advertising slogans a grandparent remembered:
GO TO WORK ON AN EGG . . . DON'T SAY VINEGAR, SAY SARSONS . . . TOP PEOPLE TAKE THE TIMES . . . LIVELY MINDS LIKE THE GUARDIAN . . . ALL HUMAN LIFE IS THERE (an old slogan for a Sunday newspaper)
A Bible
Photocopies of lengthy captions to old cartoons in Punch

A season's worth of football programmes
A letter from a husband stationed in India during the war.

A standing order is something that always applies when children are writing. Here are mine:

Children's writing experiences in school should be as much like professional writers' experiences as possible. The author Diane Samuels wrote (*The Guardian* 9 December 2008) : 'The question I have asked over and over is why what I have encountered of creative writing in schools bears so little relation to what working writers do'.

For a start, children should have their materials – notebook and pen or pencil – with them, easily available at all times. It is destructive of good writing if every time they write, a 'monitor' (dreary word) has to hand out basic materials, because often that monitor enjoys her moment of seniority and takes her time. And, because writing is an activity that should be a normal part of a class's routine, the unavailability, or the delayed availability, of its tools tells a different story: that writing is a special thing that requires rituals.

Again, treating children as working writers means not insisting that they write the date before they begin; or they underline their title (they shouldn't even be thinking of their titles at this early stage, let alone underlining it); or insisting that they (I have come across this more than once) write 'LO' [Learning Objective] at the top of the page. In one school where this was the rule, I said to the teacher 'Writers don't have to write the date before they begin, or underline their title, or write down their LO. They won't even have a clue what their LO is! Why should children have to do these things?' The reply spoke volumes: 'But this is a school'. I wanted to cry with impotent fury.

CHILDREN WRITING: MORE ON STANDING ORDERS

Another standing order!

Children should, like professional writers, have notebooks.

There is a universe of difference between an exercise book (probably a 'literacy book', or perhaps a 'jotter') and a notebook. The first is formal and administrative, and is open on any adult's (teacher's, LSA's, inspector's) demand to immediate inspection and assessment: it belongs to the school and the system.

The second is a real writing tool, a place for exploration. It is something that all writers need. It should not be marked by the teacher: indeed, children should have the right (which, in my experience, they rarely insist on) to keep it private. It probably has plain white pages, rather than institutionally lined pages; it belongs to the child/writer. An ideal notebook should be hard-backed; this makes it easier for children to write in a variety of settings.

Other connections between a professional writer's life and the children's lives as writers include times of quietness, decent space and time. And, at a basic level, children should not have to raise their hands to ask for permission to get more paper, or sharpen a pencil, or to get a spelling checked.

We are all writers. I think of the man who felt moved to scratch 'Kilroy was here' on a rock somewhere. In writing that simple three-word sentence (though it is not recorded whether he remembered his full stop) he was proclaiming his existence. When we write, whether as children or adults, we too proclaim our existence to the word. As the poet John Cotton put it:

Against the fear
of nothingness
I was here
plead all the Kilroys of this world. ('Kilroy was here',
from the book of the same title)

So children can write. They need to proclaim that 'Kilroy was here'. I always treat children as writers, even when, or especially when, they don't see themselves as such, and when other people don't. Note that the first follows on from the second: the children will believe in their abilities as much, or as little, as we do.

I would never say to a visiting writer, especially in the children's hearing, 'They can't write yet'. I say this now from the heart: it has been said to me many times, and often in Year 2 classes. If the children think – know – that you believe that, they will believe it, and they will behave like non-writers. And, as William Blake wrote in a letter, 'Neither Youth nor Childhood is Folly or Incapacity'.

CHILDREN WRITING: PROVIDING SUPPORT

Encourage 'attack'. This is when children set to with confidence. They know that they are writers: you have encouraged this belief. The pencils, or pens, or keyboards are already set for them when you lit them up with your idea: they do not have to wait for a monitor to hand out their materials. They know that writing their names and the date are secondary tasks, to be completed later if at all (as they are for professional writers). They know that they if they fill a sheet they do not have to come to you to ask for another one. They attack the task, much as I do when I am cooking, or as my neighbour does (I am watching now as I write) when he is gardening.

Children should be taught to have a go at words if they are unsure of the spellings. I do not ask them to try out words for correct spelling so that they can be checked by you! I have just spent a day in a school where the Year 3 children had been programmed to do this, and they spent more time having words checked than they did writing. Those children had been taught a writing lesson, but the support was nothing to do with writing, but with secretarial skills. And all the teacher was doing was not educational, but clerical.

And I do not ask the children to put their hand up when they need a spelling checked. Does a writer do this?

Drafting is not a matter of writing, re-writing and re-writing until something is ready for a parental inspection, or for display. Neither is it a matter of copying out until the spelling and grammar are perfect. It is (first draft) thinking, getting ideas down in note form; and (second draft) making things clearer and more vivid with arrows, crossings-out, more thinking and (third draft) of re-writing with changes.

Make it new. All clichés – birds that 'tweet prettily', lions that 'pounce on their prey', 'flowers with their sweet perfumes' – are simply evidence of a writer not thinking things through. In fact, children are not as much prone to clichés as journalists; but alerting them to the few they do use is worth doing early. Examples of clichés actually encouraged by teachers.

Some parts of speech work harder than others. Verbs make things happen. Nouns name things, as Adam did in Chapter 2 of Genesis. Verbs and nouns are muscle and bones. Adjectives and adverbs are fat. The list, often seen in classrooms, offering 'some interesting adjectives' is, quite simply, rotten advice.

All the above standing orders, when consistently applied, make a massive difference to what children can write: to their thinking, talking, reading and writing.

CHILDREN WRITING: STANDING ORDERS
FURTHERMORE

CHILDREN WRITING: COMPLEX SENTENCES

I ask children to write a sentence addressed to a kind teacher who has taught them in the past. The sentence, I insist, must have more than one part. These two parts might be connected in one of at least four ways: a 'connective', of course, or what used to be called a 'conjunction'; a preposition; a comma; or a semi-colon. Note all this technical language, not used here as part of a 'literacy' lesson, but in the process of writing.

One child wrote: 'You held my hand on the playground the day after my parents split up'. ('After' is the preposition). I showed her how she could change the feel of the sentence simply by rearranging the clauses, and by changing a few words: 'The day after my parents split up, you held my hand on the playground'. (Here, the comma is making the sentence more complex). I asked her: 'What else would you say to that teacher?' The sentence became more complex: 'The day after my parents split up, you held my hand on the playground and talked to me about all my friends' ('and', of course, being the 'connective', or 'conjunction').

Other examples from children's work in my notebooks include: 'You taught me that it was good to get muddy'. Some sentences, though the child probably doesn't fully realize the fact, reflect less well on teachers: 'You taught me that learning is everything in life when we are children, and friends are not'.

The model for these is a sentence that has survived from the New Kingdom in Ancient Egypt, c. 2000–1500 BC: 'I grew up beside you, you smote my back, and so your teaching entered my ear.' I found this in Michael Rosen's admirable if saddening anthology *The Penguin Book of Childhood* (1994).

Why not teach the lesson described above without that stricture 'to a *kind* teacher'? Why not to *any* teacher? Well, obviously, the project would be fraught with potential embarrassment, not to say distress. But I have done it often with teachers on courses, and one day, when I am confident enough of my environment, and my relationship with my colleagues, I will try it with children. In the meantime, I note what teachers have written on my courses. This adds a little shade to the pictures painted in Idea 76:

> You hit the palm of my hand with a steel ruler because I'd drilled a hole in the woodwork bench on one of those double periods I dreaded every Thursday.
>
> When I joined the choir, you told me to mime because I was a growler.
>
> When I got my sums wrong, you told me not to bother with maths, because I was good at English; I thought you were being kind, but you turned me off Maths for my lifetime.

Here is a child writing a biographical note about her little brother:

> My brother's name is Nicholas. He is 6. Sometimes he's a real menace. He flicks the houses and the hotels across the board when I am playing Monopoly. He has dark brown eyes. They sparkle and glitter when he is enjoying himself. He has a few freckles on top of his stubby little nose. He has shiny brown hair with a few waves. He has lips that are a little fat. They are bright red and his ears curl round. When he was first born he had ebony hair.

When we teach writing, we are always teaching PSME (Personal, Social and Moral Education). In other words, we are teaching both what we are, and how important our relationships are; and, more relevantly we are helping children to examine themselves and their relationships.

We are also teaching the writing of grammatical sentences, and, with some thought on the part of her teacher, it was little problem to teach this writer how to maker her biographical piece more vivid. She combined some of her simple sentences to make more complex ones. She later re-drafted her piece (on top of her first draft) like this:

> My brother Nicholas (who is six) is sometimes a real menace. He flicks the houses and the hotels across the board when I am playing Monopoly. He has dark brown eyes that sparkle and glitter when he is enjoying himself. He has a few freckles on top of his stubby little nose, shiny brown hair with a few waves, and lips that are a little fat: bright red. He has his ears curl round.

> *When he was first born he had ebony hair.*

All this was taught when the writer was re-drafting. She was learning how to write complex sentences, of course, but according to me, she was learning some things that are far more important: about her baby brother, about her relations to him, about her feelings for him, and about family lore: 'When he was first born he had ebony hair' is obviously something that her parents have told her.

CHILDREN WRITING BIOGRAPHY – CONTINUED

I ask children to do something that I have been doing in the last few weeks: to research the biography of a parent, carer, uncle, aunt or grandparent. Writing a biography, or biographical notes, involves research (a word that I like to introduce as early as possible). We have to find out about different versions of a life, much as I am doing by talking to my older half-sister, my brother, and reading material from the Ministry of Defence that is helping me to find out about my father's career in the British Army during the Second World War.

Obviously, many (though sadly not all) of them can ask questions of a parent, for example: what were you like as a child?; and then ask a grandparent about what their Dad or Mum was like as a child. Others will have more convoluted routes to follow, but there is no reason why we should not ask them to try to follow them.

Autobiography is a special case of biography. We know that an autobiography is always a large book. So, to make this exercise approachable, I talk in terms of 'autobiographical notes'. My favourite stimulus for this is a passage from *The Confessions of S. Augustine* (I try not to feel smug when I think that, up to now, I am probably the only teacher using this work with primary school children). This is my version of it, which I have adapted from the version in Michael Rosen's *Penguin Book of Childhood* (1994). I should say that, arguably, Augustine had an over-sensitive sense of his wickedness:

There was a pear-tree near the vineyard on our farm. It was loaded with pears, unpleasant to look at, and unpleasant to taste as well. Late one night the gang of boys I used to hang around with, including me, ran off and shook and shook at the tree till many of the pears fell. We had stayed out late, long after the time when our parents would have been expecting us at home. That was our usual evil habit.

We carried the pears away. We didn't eat them: we threw them at the pigs. We may have eaten a few, but the pleasure we got from this escapade was in doing something that we were not allowed to do, something that was forbidden.

I ask children to tell stories that are confessions. I make it clear that I want stories about mischief rather than wickedness: no torturing the cat, no stealing money, no bullying. After some moments of thought, they talk about this. The teachers join in the thinking as well as this telling. And then all of us (children, teachers, LSAs, anyone else who might be around – parents, the headteacher, me) write.

Once the children are mature enough – around ten or eleven, but in many cases, of course, younger, I ask them to arrange their writing like this, in three paragraphs. If I feel they will be co-operative, I ask the adults to do this, too:

Introduction: this means setting the scene – the room or outdoor place, the season, who they were with (or were they alone?), the weather, what had been going on before. This section may include their first thoughts about the mischief they are about to tell the reader about.

The main act, with as many details as they can pack in, even if some of them don't seem to matter at the moment – they may matter more later.

The consequences.

I get the children to recast their story in the *present tense*. Note how much this activity, like the next, can make children familiar with two basic terms of English grammar:

> I am out in my garden sitting staring up into the sky, bored. I can't think what to do. An idea strikes me. There in the middle of the garden is a swingball. I start hitting it one way and the other.
>
> Unfortunately my sister comes out and says 'Can I play?' But I say 'No, I like playing on my own'. But she doesn't take any notice of me. She says something like 'You can't stop me'. That makes me angry, very angry. I was playing happily till she came out. I tell her she can play after me. She is being really horrible, so I lose my temper and throw the bat. By accident it hits her on the hand and I break her finger so she has to go to hospital.
>
> And I get told off. My mum says the police might come, just to warn me, so I cry.

AUTOBIOGRAPHY: CONFESSIONS CONTINUED

And I ask the children to put the story in the *third person*, adding another basic term, and giving them opportunities to add new details that can be made up – make it a story! – and perhaps to add or change some phrases. I had mentioned to the children the power of short sentences:

It was a bright summer's day. Jennie was out in her garden sitting staring up into the clear blue sky. She couldn't think what to do. She tried reading a book and a comic in a deckchair, watching the clouds drift by, and she didn't want her mother to ask her to help with making the tea. She was bored.

An idea struck her. There in the middle of the garden was the swingball on its metal pole and two little bats. She stood. Stretched. Picked up the bat. Slowly, she started hitting it one way and then the other with a bat. But soon her sister Tracy came out and asked 'Can I play?' But Jennie wanted to play on her own, and she said 'No, I like playing on my own. Go away'. But Tracy didn't take any notice of her. She said something like 'You can't stop me'. She grabbed the other bat. She started swinging it at the ball.

That made Jennie angry, very angry. She had been playing happily till her horrible sister came out! Why couldn't she go back indoors? Why couldn't she just leave her alone? She was always interfering. Jennie told her she could play later. But Tracy was being really horrible, so Jennie really lost her rag. She threw the bat.

It hit Tracy on the hand. She burst into tears, and sat on the grass, holding the bad hand with the other one. The bat had broken her finger, so she had to go to hospital. And Jennie got told off.

Later her mum said the police might come, just to frighten her, so she cried.

This exercise, in all three stages – past tense, present tense, third person – can be used for other memories.

I get the children to find out what their parents, carers etc remember about the same event. When they come to school on a later day, they write the story again, including new details that they have discovered from their families.

One curiosity that the children will discover, not for the last time in their lives, is that different people see and remember events in different ways: an important lesson.

CONFESSIONS CONTINUED: DIFFERENT VERSIONS

WRITING A NOVEL: FIRST CHAPTERS

In an ideal world, I can envisage a ten- or eleven-year-olds writing a novel over a school year. Of course, the constraints of the rest of school life, both those that are genuinely educational and those that are mere schooling – tests and preparation for them and the like – are going to get in the way. But I have taught children in September to write the first chapter of a novel, and then hoped that they might continue the project over the school year.

I explain that, when we write stories, we often want to make things happen too soon. I ask the children to think of a central character, and then to describe a room where their central character lives or works. The details of this room are going to tell the reader as much as possible about the character's life. I ask them, what objects are in the room? describe the décor – especially the colours and fabrics of things is there any sound in the room? describe the room in a way that tells us how organized/disorganized, how happy/unhappy, the character is. What is in the room to suggest his or her personal history? What are the character's interests or even obsessions? Don't tell us what they are: show us. One child wrote this, with its faintly chilling ending. Notice the way she developed the dust and clock themes:

I stood in an old house by an entrance to a room. I thought I could hear the house creak. I pushed open the door. A heap of dust fell out. I stood back and let it pour out. Once I had stopped coughing, I went into the room. It was so old and dusty my thoughts seemed to echo around it.

I noticed a distinctive feature in a corner. It appeared to be the only thing in the room not covered by a three-centimetre layer of dust. It was very well cared-for compared to the rest of the room.

It was an old clock dated 1795. As I moved near to it, more things became visible through the thick clouds of dust. There were carriage clocks, grandfather clocks, fob-watches and all sorts.

I swept all the dust away from a corner of a mahogany table. There was a book. I opened it, and on the middle of the first page in big old-fashioned writing it said 'Repair Record 1783'.

The book was old and fragile, so I delicately turned a page. And there was a person with the same name as me.

The startling ending was all her own; though her use of a thesaurus is evident in the list of time pieces.

Almost all the best picture books are short stories. Examples are *In the Night Kitchen* and *Where the Wild Things Are* by Maurice Sendak, and a book I have referred to in both Foundation Stage and Key Stage 1: *Tiger in the Snow!* by Nick Butterworth. These books are also poetry, in their use of pattern, rhyme, metaphor and simile, and in their originality and genius. Most of the children I work with have books like these in their experience.

I ask them to write a short story in exactly 50 words. I collect, with their help, different genres: suspense, detective, school stories, mystery, romance . . . I suggest that short sentences, especially at the beginning, draw the reader in; that many great stories leave something unexplained or even, as in the following example, undescribed:

A Death

The house was silent. The dark crept into every corner. Meg's eyes shone brightly in her cat basket. She stretched, uncurled. Meg pawed her pillow and went to sleep again. In the morning she ate and went outside. Meg was deaf and didn't hear the car. The driver wasn't looking.

There is group of eight- and nine-year-olds sitting in front of 'The Supper at Emmaus' by Caravaggio in the National Gallery in London. They have been looking silently at the painting for some time, and the teacher introduces a notion that they are obviously familiar with, the 'hook phrase'.

Then the children write in hardback notebooks. Later, again with their permission (nobody withholds it), I look over some of what they have written:

> What I can see in this room is darkness all around the edges and bright light on the white tablecloth and on a man's face. He is looking down, he has pointed one hand out. Another man has stretched his arms out sideways. He has a shell on his jacket. One man is about to get out of his chair. There is a shadow on the wall . . .

I have used this picture with children myself, but with reproductions. It is a far more powerful experience for the children in the National now, as they are now, staring at the artist's brush-strokes.

I never tell the children the story of a picture until they have studied it. This one is a based on the Gospel of St Luke, chapter 24, verses 13–32, especially verses 30–31: '. . . he took bread, and blessed it, and brake it, and gave it to them. And . . . they knew him . . .'

It sheds light on our task as teachers when we attack a task we have set the children. First, it shows how difficult it can be, and how well children, fresher to the world's experience than we are, manage. And second – assuming we write alongside the children – it shows them that writing isn't something done only by children in classrooms and professional writers; that is useful for us, as well.

I tried writing in response to this picture, looking at a reproduction I have of it at home which is propped up on my desk (though I have seen it dozens of times in London):

The man in the middle is by some years the youngest of the four figures. His hair hangs in brown curls, and is almost feminine in its appearance. A shadow – the Italian waiter or the young man himself? – it isn't easy to see where the light is coming from – lies on the wall behind him. A much older man on the right, balding, grizzled, red-nosed, spreads his arms wide, like a boastful angler talking about the fish that got away. His right hand seems too big. He wears a shell – a badge of pilgrimage. He is old and tough, and his friend on the left, rising out his chair, has a tear in the elbow of his right sleeve. They are living hard lives. Despite the bread, the fowl, the wine, the fruit, the cleanliness of everything, these are poor men. I have seen carafes of wine like this one dozens of time in Italy. The brightness falls on four places: the old man's left sleeve, the table cloth, the waiter's cap and arm, and on the young man, especially on his smooth unlined forehead. He is the centre of the picture.

You might try your hand at a poem. Here's one of mine about a famous painting, 'A Country Wedding' by Pieter Bruegel the Elder. I've tried to use all my senses:

Oh the noise! the clatter
of plates on tables, the songs,
the jokes, the laughter, the smells

of burning meat, of ale spilled, of
coarse wine –

                  I shuffle along
the floor at my auntie's wedding
and eat myself nearly sick.

I will snooze through the afternoon
in my father's arms, till I wake
to 'Show me the way to go home'. [sung in Dutch by
my Uncle Pieter]

The children whom I observed in the National Gallery were silent as they looked at the Caravaggio and wrote. Conventionally, silence is required in classrooms either for administrative reasons, or because the noise has risen beyond the teacher's tolerance level. This was a different silence. The teacher hadn't felt the need to impose it. Instead, it arose from her carefully built relationship with the children, from the atmosphere in the gallery, and from the nature of the task itself.

Most writers need silence, not because someone is taking the register, or checking what they plan for lunch, or whether they have free dinners. They need it to help them think, feel, concentrate. I am dubious about those who say that they work to the accompaniment of Radio 3 or Radio 4 – have they no sense of rhythm? Aren't they aware of the clash between what they are listening to and what they are writing, both in terms of rhythm and meaning?

Children are writers. I usually tell them that when I clap my hands, the classroom will stop being a classroom, and become a study where 20-odd writers are writing; and therefore it will be silent. Even if this silence only lasts 15 minutes, it helps them to get started. It serves that neglected need (because progress in it is immeasurable) to teach children to think.

Some writers – I am one of them – treasure the results of moments when we show something we are working on to a sympathetic, but still critical, friend. But I don't find such friends easy to find. 'Lovely, Fred', most potential 'editing friends' say. 'There's a full stop missing on page 48, but otherwise it's fine.' 'Help me make it better!' I want to shout.

Children in classrooms, on the other hand, are surrounded by potential editing friends who will discuss matters more important than missing punctuation marks, though they will identify those, too.

I ask children to read out a piece of their writing they're pleased with to a friend. Importantly, there is no compulsion here. They may have written something they'd prefer to keep quiet about. I also tell children that they must listen to each other respectfully, and with 100 per cent attention.

Later on I ask the children to read all of what they've been writing to each other in pairs. I think it is best if each child reads his or her writing twice. The first time, the partner will listen in silence, and the second time he or she will ask questions and make suggestions.

I train children to query words like 'bird' and 'tree' – 'What kind of bird?' 'What tree do you mean? Evergreen or deciduous? Small or large?' I train them, too, to watch out for vague words: 'nice' of course. But 'lovely', 'beautiful' and 'horrible' never punch their weight. Neither does the vague noun 'prey': 'Deer? Zebra? Worm?'

This helps the children to become careful writers and attentive critics.

Writing in the intense way that poetry demands will help children, and anyone else, to write with a due regard for words, facts, truth (insofar as those concepts can be disentangled).

Teaching poetry helps children, like nothing else can, about the weight words can carry: how the adjective 'nice' is a feather, never worth writing; and the noun 'apple' (think of the Garden of Eden and Snow White) resonates throughout our culture; how the word verb/ noun 'lie' has different meanings; how metaphor and simile work.

Writing poetry teaches the writer to face the truth. As much as you can't *pray* a lie, you can't (as the poet Les Murray puts it in his poem 'Poetry and Religion' in *Collected Poems* 1991) *'poe'* one either. You can't be dishonest in a poem. You must get it true.

Grammar is best taught through creative writing. It swims into the lesson naturally, rather than being imposed from without, or even separated from writing altogether. Poetry has a reputation among some for being free of all the constraints of grammar, but this is not so. Grammatical words below include 'preposition', 'prepositional phrase', 'article', 'definite', 'indefinite', 'sentence' and 'noun'. Throughout this book, I have also included others: 'connective', 'conjunction', 'noun', 'verb', 'adjective', 'adverb' and many others. The consistent use of such terms in our teaching of writing will do more for learning about them than any lesson labelled with them.

A story: a Year 6 teacher is 'teaching adverbs'. He explains that they qualify verbs, and demonstrates this on the whiteboard thus: he writes 'I ran to the beach quickly', underlining the adverb *quickly*, and double-underlining the '-*ly*'. 'The adverb "quickly"' he explains, 'qualifies the verb "ran"'. He does the same with the sentence 'I walked to the bank slowly'. He then asks the children if they can think of a sentence with an adverb, ending in '-ly'.

And a child offers 'I ate my breakfast, muesli'.

Who's talking the better sense?

POETRY: PREPOSITIONS

I divide the whiteboard into three parts with vertical lines.

In the first part, I collect prepositions from the children: 'inside', 'outside', 'behind', 'before', 'under', 'between' as well as prepositional phrases: 'in front of', 'next to', and so on.

In the second part, I collect nouns with either the definite or the indefinite article: 'the window', 'the frame', 'a mirror', 'a tree', 'a hill', 'a mountain' and so on. I emphasize words that have a kind of resonance: all the above, and 'sea', 'lake', 'river' and others. Such words will probably (though not certainly) work better than 'computer', 'television' etc.

I ask the children: Build the beginning of a sentence of your own, starting with a preposition and a noun from each of the two groups. I suggest that they ignore common sense.

Children have offered:

Behind the mountain . . .
Over the sea. . .
Through the window . . .
Under the river . . .

Then I ask the children to complete each sentence.

Now simply show the children how to make a poem (or is it prose? Who cares as long as they are learning?) using an element from the first two groups, and a conclusion of their own, which might contain, or be introduced with, another preposition (1), a participle (2 and 3) or a simile (4).

Inside the girl's head is a dream of days under the sun. (1)
Over the sand there is a green rock pool with crabs scuttling. (2)
Inside the girl's head is a unicorn bowing his horn to her. (3)

In the field are the names of friends like a daisy
chain. (4)

Again, common sense is not the main thing. Children
should go where their first phrase leads them

POETRY AND PHILOSOPHY: QUESTIONS

I write up 'philo' and explain that it means 'friend' in Ancient Greek. Then I write up 'sophy': 'knowledge', or 'wisdom'. Put the two together, and we get 'philosophy', which means friendship with knowledge. 'We are going to do philosophy now. Please close your eyes, and think of a question you'd love to know the answer to, but you know you never will. It mustn't be a question you could look up in a book . . . and googling won't help much either.'

As their hands begin to go up I say, 'When you've got one question, keep your eyes closed and your hands down, and think of another . . . and another.'

After about two minutes, many of them will be dying to share questions. I did this the other week, and the first one came from a six-year-old boy: 'How did the space-time continuum begin?'

When the invention begins to flag, I ask the children to close their eyes again, and think of more questions, possibly containing the following keywords: 'God', 'peace', 'love', 'hate', 'war'.

Among the most striking questions asked have been (all from six-year-olds) 'dos god bleeve in me' (no, I didn't correct spelling and punctuation), 'How can I tell if a man is evil or not?' and (this, in varying forms, almost always comes up) 'Why do we die?'

When a child accumulates 12 questions, I ask her to underline the best one. Then she writes her questions out again, repeating the best one every fourth line: a philosophical poem!

This lesson brings out into the open concerns that all children have, and allows them to reflect on them. `

dos god bleeve in me

Note that this idea provokes questions:

   about religion
   about growth
   about family life
   about love
   about death

I try to give the children, whenever the other pressures in time permit, a long period of discussion. It is best, I find, if this takes place about a week after the first session.

POETRY AND PHILOSOPHY: QUESTIONS (CONTINUED)

Ou est le cauchemar
Que je deteste
Quand j'avais cinq ans?
Dormant dans mon lit.

Ten-year-old

Thirty years ago, most teachers taught as though children with English as a second, third or fourth language were at a disadvantage. We now know that the opposite is true.

Wes Magee has a poem that begins 'Where's the rattle / I shook / when I was one / lost'. I often use this poem with children to help them construct their own stanzas. In one school, I found a Swiss girl who, the teacher told me, had three languages. She wrote her first stanza in English:

Where's the nightmare
I hated
When I was five?
Sleeping in my bed.

And then translated it into French, as above. She then asked me: 'Would you like me to translate this into German?'

I ask the children what objects might send a valentine to what other objects. Suggestions come thick and fast, nearly always provoked by objects in the classroom. These are not especially interesting: 'The pen to the paper', for example. I say, let's go (in our minds) outside, and immediately a kind of resonance arrives: 'The wind to the trees . . . the grass to the field . . .' I suggest: Let's go to the seaside . . . to a foreign country . . . to somewhere else in the solar system.

I ask the children to write their lines down in a list like this, punctuating correctly with a comma after the first two lines, 'and' at the beginning of the fourth, and a full stop at the end:

> The waves to the shore,
> The pyramids to the Sphinx,
> Saturn to its rings
> And Paris to the Eiffel Tower.

And so on.

At this point I show the children that some of the final words in these lines are easy to rhyme: For example, I ask, what rhymes with 'shore'? When the child offers, say, 'more', or 'door', or 'floor', I ask him or her to think of things that might send a valentine to one of those things.

I might get 'The ceiling to the floor'. I now suggest that that line will be line four in a stanza, and that the 'shore' line (so to speak) will be line two:

> (2) The waves to the shore,
> (4) The ceiling to the floor.

And then I ask them to pick two lines from their list – they must not rhyme – that they are pleased with. These will become lines 1 and 3:

> The garden to the flowers
> The waves to the shore,
> The gate to the pathway
> And the ceiling to the floor.

I explain that this is a 'quatrain' (linking this word up with 'quadrilateral', 'quadrangle' and 'quadbike') that rhyme abcb. This surprises and delights them, and they readily write more quatrains.

Repeat the exercise, but this time each quatrain must focus on a chosen area: music, for example.

> The drum to the drumstick,
> The bow to the hand,
> The keys to the piano
> And the leader to the band.

Or, with boys in mind, sport:

> The football to the ball,
> The rider to the horse,
> The jumper to the pit
> And the runner to the course.

One keen fisherman wrote:

> The rod to the line,
> The bait to the fish,
> The patience to the waiting
> And the salmon to the dish.

POETRY: QUATRAINS AND VALENTINES (CONTINUED)

FIVE SENSES

As I have suggested in Idea 40, alerting children to the five senses always revitalizes writing. Children (and most writers) are customarily attuned to sight and hearing, so I usually emphasize smell and touch. Taste, I always thought, can be limiting. But my 11-year-old son wrote:

Dad

I taste your taste
when I taste a thick-topped mushroom pizza.
It reminds me
of me and you in Egypt
looking at the pelicans.

I listen to you
when I hear keys jangling
down on to the sideboard
where the phone is
or when I hear jazz swing
on a radio.

I see you in a book of W H Auden poems
or when I see the stereo
left unattended in a corner
or a clean shirt
just out of the wash.

John Lynch, Daniel's teacher at the time, told me that he had asked the children to think hard about someone they loved in terms of their senses.

When I tried out his idea later, children wrote:

My mum smells like a rose.
My dad's arm is like smooth paper.
My granddad's arm is like a rough pillow.
My dad's eyes are like dark chocolate.
My mum's hair is like black oil.

My book has almost turned full circle. What delighted children in my company when they were at Foundation Stage still delights them now. The other picture books that they had read to them by me and their teachers still delight them. Often, indeed, they have read those books to themselves, revisiting that tiger and those frightened chickens, and Angry Max and his wild things. So I read those picture books to them again, often in that lovely 20-minute period between tidying up and going home, which should be a calm making-up of quarrels, a re-assertion of the friendships you all have for each other.

A writing idea for the last day of the summer term:

Lie in bed late	lounging and lolling about	
Eat eggs and bacon	for breakfast at eleven	
Sprawl on the lawn	with a long glass of lemonade	
Eat salad and seafood	travel the town tee-shirted	
Green mates	grinning with freedom	Bowl
Bash those bails down	belt the leather ball	
Bouncing to the boundary	bounce bounce	Bring
A take-away home	parathas and poppadoms	
Talk about treats	sunlight through trees and sand	
Sleep in deep silence between sheets	Dream	
Fred Sedgwick		

I ask the children to note the alliteration. It based on an Anglo-Saxon model. I ask them to celebrate the end of the school year by writing a poem in alliterating lines like this about the joys to come in the summer holidays.

The counting-out rhyme that gave me my title for these sections is:

Eeny feeny figgery feg
Deely dyly ham and egg
Calico back and stony rock
Arlum barlum BASH!

Ahlberg, J. and Ahlberg, A. (1983) *Peepo*. London: Penguin.

Augustine St and Pin-Coffin, R. S. (2005) *Confessions*. London: Penguin.

Browne, A. (1993) *Helping Children to Write*. London: Paul Chapman.

Butterworth, N. (2006) *Tiger in the Snow*. London: HarperCollins.

Causley, C. (1992) *The Collected Poems*. London: Macmillan.

Causley, C. (1996) *The Collected Poems for Children*. London: Macmillan.

Clayton, M. (1992) *Leonardo da Vinci: The Anatomy of Man*. London: Little Brown.

Cotton, J. (1975) *Kilroy Was Here: Poems 1970–74*. London: Chatto & Windus.

Dickens, C. (1999) *David Copperfield*. Oxford: Oxford paperbacks.

Dixon P (undated) *Display in the Primary School*. Winchester: Dixon.

Grahame, K. (2009) *The Wind in the Willows*. Annotated edition. New York: W. W. Norton.

Hughes, T. (1989) *How the Whale Became and Other Stories*. London: Faber and Faber.

Hughes, T. (2005) *The Collected Poems for Children*. London: Faber and Faber.

Jerome, Jerome K. (1999) *Three Men in a Boat*. London: Penguin Books.

Kerr, J. (2006) *Six Stores about Mog*. London: HarperCollins.

Mathe, J. (1980) *Leonardo's Inventions* trans. David MacRae. Geneva: Miller Graphics.

Murray, L. (1991) *Collected Poems*. Manchester: Carcarnet Press.

Opie, I. and Opie, P. (1959) *The Lore and Language of Schoolchildren*. Oxford: Oxford University Press.

Popham, A. E. (1994) *The Drawings of Leonardo da Vinci*. London: Pimlico.

Pullman, P. (2007 [2000]) *The Amber Spyglass. His Dark Materials.* New York: Random House Inc.

Rosen, M. (1994) *The Penguin Book of Childhood.* London: Penguin.

Sedgwick, F. (2000) *Writing to Learn: Poetry and Literacy across the Primary School Curriculum* London: RoutledgeFalmer.

Sedgwick, F. (2001) *Teaching Literacy: A Creative Approach.* London: Continuum.

Sedgwick, F. (2002) *Enabling Children's Learning through Drawing.* London: David Fulton Publishers.

Sedgwick, F. (2003) *Teaching Poetry.* London: Continuum.

Sendak, M. (1963) *Where the Wild Things Are.* London: Red Fox.

Sendak, M. (1970) *In the Night Kitchen.* New York: HarperCollins.

Tizard, B. (1986) *Young Children Learning Talking and Thinking at Home and at School.* London: Fontana.

Vernon, P. E. (ed.) (1970) 'Creative Writers and Day-Dreaming', quoted in *Creativity.* Harmondsworth: Penguin Books.

Wells, G. (1994). *The Meaning Makers.* London: Hodder and Stoughton.